CW00588644

Drop Out
And Get Schooled

The Case For Thinking Twice About College

Patrick Bet-David

With

Thomas N. Ellsworth

FIRST EDITION

Print
ISBN: 978-0-9974410-2-4

eBook
ISBN: 978-0-9974410-4-8

DEDICATION

To all the entrepreneurs who had the courage
to drop out of college and get schooled on their own.

CONTENTS

ACKNOWLEDGMENTS 9

INTRODUCTION 11

PROLOGUE...15

1. WHY WE GO TO COLLEGE 21

2. WHO SHOULD GO TO COLLEGE?......................39

3. WHO SHOULD NOT GO TO COLLEGE?...........47

4. THE BUSINESS OF COLLEGE 65

5. BEFORE YOU DROP OUT… 77

6. WHAT SHOULD BE ADDED TO COLLEGE?...87

7. HOW TO PROCESS YOUR DECISION 97

8. A SAMPLE CONVERSATION................................101

9. WHAT NOW? JOIN THE REVOLUTION!........115

ADDENDUM: DROPOUT HALL OF FAME 117

ABOUT THE AUTHORS 123

SPEAKING REQUESTS..127

END NOTES 129

ACKNOWLEDGMENTS

The tradition of including acknowledgments is long and distinguished. It does seem, however, a bit redundant to continually tip the hat to those who exhibit patience and tolerance on a daily basis, even as new projects, such as this book, come to life.

I'll do it this way: You know who you are and your work and support are appreciated more than you can possibly know.

I'd also like to acknowledge the people who sent supportive emails and made positive comments on social media about this topic. Many of you made fantastic points that you may see reflected in some way within this book. Thank you for stating your case.

Thank you also to those who wrote me in defense of college and were critical of my position. More than one of you pointed out that the average salary for Ph.D.'s, MBA's and bachelor's degree recipients was several times higher, on average than those who did not attend college. As you will read in the following chapters, my question is not if college works – it does – but for whom. I believe the current system is, in many ways, broken, and the concept of education comprises a broader continuum. I am an autodidact, that is, I am predominantly self-taught.

My sincere hope is that this book creates a debate that leads to discussions at kitchen tables and positive encouragement for those who find themselves learning outside of the "normal" or "traditional" system. Too many students drop out of school with overwhelming student loan debt while others find work in a profession that doesn't utilize their degree. Tell me again, how is that good?

Lastly a big thank you to all the researchers and reporters who assembled the reports and articles cited in this book. That should cover everyone. Thanks to all!

INTRODUCTION

The purpose of this book is NOT to declare that higher education is a terrible thing. It's absolutely not. BUT, learning can and does take place in many forms. I've read 1,200 books in the last 15 years and understand firsthand that you CAN educate yourself. Many entrepreneurs do so and go on to make a very real impact in their part of an industry sector, or a massive impact that changes the world itself.

There are important professions that require a formal education – such as medicine. I praise God for the skilled cardiologists that attended whatever university that would have them and studied under whichever faculty that trained them to perform miraculous heart procedures such as the one that saved my dad's life. There is no debate that a college education is vital to certain specialized professions, particularly those in science and medicine. Also, I join my fellow Americans who certainly don't want a self-taught nuclear physicist building a new bomb for the military, especially if the lab is in our town. Those professions require not only a college education but sufficient time to sober-up following the college experience itself.

But is a trip to college vital to ALL professions? No way!

Before I go any further, I am compelled to step back and make an important point about high school. Never, never, never, never, never drop out of high school or take the GED (General Equivalency Diploma). Did I say NEVER? A high school is a place for young people to develop core skills intellectually and relationally. It's also an accomplishment to be celebrated. High school dropouts are four times more likely than college graduates to be unemployed. Thus, stopping the formal educational process, even at a horrible public school in some troubled downtown area, is something I am against with every bit of emphasis that I can muster.

Those first 18 years are a time of critical personal development, and the maturing process doesn't stop at 18. For example, our government (run by a drunken legislature if recent newspaper headlines are any indication) believes young people should not be permitted to drink until they are 21 – that's three more years after graduating high school at 18. But the same legislature thinks that an 18-year-old is old enough to go to war and use multi-million-dollar machinery to kill people you don't know but apparently not old enough to sit around and have a beer afterward and talk about the people you just killed. Think about that one for a moment. On second thought, don't. Where was I?

I am compelled to initiate a dialogue about college and the uniquely personal decision-making process that each person must undertake before they make a final decision. So, let's talk about WHO should go to college and WHO should think twice about it as well as WHY dropping out is the right choice for some people.

Most importantly, we will examine HOW to process all of those questions in the first place. As you will see, I am going to pull in articles, blogs and opinions as well as present my point of view in an attempt to start an honest dialogue.

Sound processing leads to a good decision and that, my friends, *IS* the purpose of this book.

Let's begin the journey.

- PBD

PATRICK BET-DAVID with THOMAS N. ELLSWORTH

DROP OUT AND GET SCHOOLED

PROLOGUE

Thomas N. Ellsworth

Monday, October 15, 1984

It often takes a perfectly avoidable human tragedy to get our attention. That was the case for me on what started out as a typical day in Los Angeles in the fall of 1984.

It was the fall semester of my junior year at California State University Northridge, and I ("Tom") was grinding through elective courses which seemed absolutely pointless. I mean, why on Earth do they force a business major to take Astronomy (pun intended) while pursuing a marketing and business degree? The goal was to get a Bachelor of Science in Business Administration and secure a job in sales or marketing. The paradigm that drove that goal was one that I lived under since attending high school in Boca Raton, Florida: without a college degree, your future would have a very low ceiling.

During high school, I worked at a restaurant as a chef's assistant. Somehow I avoided being a busboy and secured a job working with the lead chefs in the kitchen of a prominent local steakhouse. This job also afforded me the opportunity to enjoy the Florida sunshine during the day.

My passion wasn't surfing, but some of my friends surfed, and

I would go to the beach from time to time to enjoy the sand and waves just the same. Surfers inevitably damaged their surfboards thanks to rocks, coral or the occasional bump into a fellow surfer. These are called "dings," and dings in a fiberglass surfboard would need to be patched so that saltwater would not rot the foam inside the board and, importantly, fiberglass slivers did not cut your hands or feet. Local surf shops sold repair kits containing putty or epoxy that did little more than simply cover the ding. The material was typically yellowish and turned an ugly brown after exposure to the sun. The alternative was silver duct tape which was effective but ugly. Surfers carefully selected their boards, and many had elaborate color or artwork. The original beauty of the surfboard was lost as the dings and patches multiplied over time.

I wondered why surfboards could not be restored in a high-quality way, the same way professional body shops repair cars. The answer was that, yes, they could be – but it required locating a professional surfboard builder and shipping or driving the board to that location. Typically, only badly damaged boards were repaired this way – because it wasn't cheap and it took a lot of time which meant you could not use your board to surf. Thus, the minor dings were simply patched with cheap kits.

There was no Google and no Internet, so I performed research by asking surf shops about surfboards. Then I asked paint stores about fiberglass and resin. One person referred me to another, and before long I had amassed quite a bit of knowledge. Without realizing it, this was the education phase of my first entrepreneurial pursuit. I bought small quantities of the materials and repaired a couple of dings on a friend's board. I experimented with various techniques to repair various types of dings. I learned how to make patches of any type and, more importantly, make them look as good as new.

Rather than walk the beach and evangelize my newfound skill to surfers, I went to local surf shops and simply offered to do ding-repair with free pickup and delivery to and from the surf shop. This enabled the shop owners to earn a little money off dings, and it was great for the local surfers who could get quick, high-quality and affordable ding repair. I picked up surfboards in the morning and dropped them off in the late afternoon. I made good money, much more than minimum wage, and launched my first venture.

After a busy year of ding repair that saw me commandeer my parents' garage, it was clear that ding repair was not going to be a long-term pursuit. Oh, and my dad evicted me from the garage as a means to encourage me to move on to college. That led me back to Los Angeles where I enrolled at CSUN and pursued a marketing degree.

On the road to that degree, Monday, October 15, 1984, began as a day in college typically did. My morning routine was to arrive on campus an hour early for my 8:00 AM class. This allowed me to avoid morning traffic and gave me the opportunity to sit in the cafeteria on the rooftop of the Sierra South building and talk with friends over coffee.

I parked in the student lot, hopped out of my car, slung my backpack over my shoulder and walked towards Sierra South. It was 75 degrees and breezy, pretty much as it is every fall day in L.A. I was thinking about nothing in particular as I enjoyed the quiet solitude of the morning.

My morning dramatically changed as I turned the corner and was stunned by the horrifying sight of a body partially covered by a blanket. Campus police officers and a man with a black jacket that said "Coroner" on the back were standing over the body and jotting in notebooks as they looked up at Sierra tower. There were no blinking lights, no paramedics, no fire department and no Los Angeles Police – they were not needed as the truth was obvious. The student under the blanket in the puddle of blood had jumped from the tower to his death.

After I had taken a couple of deep breaths, my first thought was simply, "What could have possibly been so bad?" I stood there silently for a few minutes – not gawking at the scene just staring into the distance. I eventually turned away, gathered my thoughts and went upstairs to meet my friends.

The normal routine of mindless morning chatter was replaced with a deeply thoughtful and appropriately somber discussion punctuated by a mixture of sadness and helpless frustration. None of my coterie of friends personally knew the student that committed suicide, but all felt the same way, and it was summed up in a simple sentence, "*Nothing* was so bad that he needed to jump to his death."

The lecture in my 8:00 class was merely background noise to the dialogue in my mind. I couldn't stop thinking about a fellow student that I didn't even know.

The next day, the campus newspaper covered the grisly story and indicated the student had been depressed and even sought help with anxiety. I thought, "How did they find out so much less than 24 hours after his death but no one did, or could do, anything in the months before?"

It was tragic that no one he reached out to had been able to help him. I wondered about the source of his anxiety. A front-page article that accompanied the story carried an ominous headline: "Pressure to perform can lead to college suicides." Link: http://hyperurl.co/jx9q39

When I read that story, I felt even worse than I did the previous morning when it happened. Questions rolled back and forth in my mind, "Do 18 to 21-year-old people feel so much pressure that they take themselves out? They have 80 percent of their life in front of them." Students that I did not know personally died that year in car accidents or were diagnosed with cancer, but this one death left me numb. Perhaps I was youthfully naïve or simply came from a positive angle that left me believing there were always options in life and no catastrophe was insurmountable.

No, I didn't know the student who jumped that day in 1984, but I wished that I did. I would have reminded him of a simple truth: *Nothing about college was so big that poor grades or even dropping out were worth the ultimate sacrifice.* I was convinced that there are always other paths in life, and yes, they might be tough hikes. Sometimes you can even invent your own options. I was living proof of that because not so many months before that day I wasn't even in college – I was repairing surfboards in my parents' garage.

Over 30 years later, it still upsets me to think about it.

1

WHY WE GO TO COLLEGE

Generational Habit, Tradition and Peer Pressure

An interviewer once asked Malcolm X where he went to college.

His answer was simple: "Books."

Education is broken, and most graduates are broke. This is the new reality in the greatest country in the world. We are a mob of robots merely following our programming.

It's time to rethink the social assumptions, traditions, familial influence and peer-pressure that comprises the decision calculus that leads so many to "just go" to college.

In this book, I'll make a case for why I believe 80 percent of college students should drop out of college or not go in the first place. According to current stats,[i] only 60 percent will graduate, meaning 40 percent will drop out anyway. My sense is most people (students and their parents) are reluctant or even afraid to make this argument because it flies in the face of the century-long robotic march to the tune of "go to college and get a good job." Why haven't more people questioned this?

There are parents who are influenced or forced by peer pressure and societal norms to finance their childrens' college education, many doing so with their retirement savings or, worse, second mortgages on their homes. This, mind you, without any guarantees that it'll produce the desired results for *their particular son or daughter*. That is simply insane to me.

As a parent of three, I understand the importance of investing in your childrens' future, but I also believe we must first ask ourselves about the final product and by-products our current educational system is producing.

Many will disagree with my argument, and to those, my challenge is before they throw the book in the trash or the fireplace, let me make the case. If it doesn't make any sense to you, I encourage you to light this book up. To be transparent, I want you to know that I am a college drop out and my friend Tom Ellsworth, whom I asked to co-author this book with me, has a 4-year undergraduate degree, an MBA and is an adjunct professor of an MBA program.

I did schooling somewhat backward. Let me start at the beginning. As a kid who grew up in a broken family with a divorced and single mother doing her best to raise me, it's no surprise that I became very rebellious. Most Middle Eastern families want or expect their kids to become an engineer, a doctor or an attorney. Me? Well, I ended up joining the Army after high school. It was pretty obvious no university was interested in a student who was rebellious, got an 880 on the SAT and managed only a 1.8 GPA. Those numbers typically point to trouble, maybe even a perfect candidate for prison!

Society influenced me to believe that I was not meant to do anything special with my life. My high school guidance counselors would speak to me as if I was a project on which they had to work. They had great intentions, but they put me in the box labeled "future failures in life." I remember one sit-down meeting with one of my counselors. I'll call her Mrs. K for privacy purposes. She told me "Son, I feel sorry for your parents. I would also have had multiple heart attacks if I was your father." How encouraging is that? I laugh about it now but back then my father DID have a major heart attack that almost cost him his life.

We currently have a highly complex multi-variate social system that influences and guides approximately 30 percent of high school freshmen on a path to ultimately graduate from college. Perhaps this is thanks to the rote preparation or some encouragement from parents and teachers or, one assumes, some idea of what they plan on majoring in school. On the other hand, perhaps it's none of those.

The data compiled and announced from 2013 to 2015 looks like this (please see endnote "i" for citations) for a batch of 100 "average" high school students:

100 will start high school in grade 9

80 will graduate (20 drop outs)

53 will enroll in college (27 get no further education)

30 will graduate from college (23 drop outs)

So, approximately 30% of the students who stepped foot into high school as freshmen will graduate from college. That's all? Yep, that's all.

As long as we are talking about these "lucky 30," it needs to be pointed out that they are also graduating with more than just a paper degree. These happy graduates will also be holding a piece of paper that says they owe an inordinate amount of debt.

In fact, This according to research compiled by Mark Kantrowitz, a student financial aid policy expert, and publisher of Edvisors.com, the class of 2015 is carrying the most student debt in U.S. history, an average of $35,000 EACH.

Don't feel bad class of 2015; your record debt will almost certainly be exceeded by the class of 2016 (and it's not a record you want to brag about).

Oh wait, let's get back to the other 70 who don't graduate college. Here's the math on those 70:

20 will drop out of high school

27 will graduate high school but not go to college

22 will drop out of college

What do those 70 do? Do they ever get educated?

As for me, what did I do? I joined the Army. After serving with the 101st Airborne and learning a trade, I had to make a choice about re-enlisting. At the moment of decision, one of my good friends, Kogan Allahverdian called me the night before my re-enlisting ceremony (another six years) to ask me why I was staying. This was a very strange evening. I had just gotten off the phone with my father who was very excited about me re-enlisting because the Army gave me everything I had asked for my next assignment; special forces, Army Ranger school, and placement on base in Vicenza, Italy. That's an exciting place for a single guy who's filled with enough hormonal energy to start a small city by himself!

Kogan spoke to me for an hour at midnight and said he wanted to make an argument for why I should get out of the Army. I asked him, "What am I going to do? I don't have any special skills. There are no jobs in the civilian world for someone who's high-level expertise consists of firing a semi-automatic weapon and repairing Humvees." Now, truth be told, I learned fast and was a pretty good mechanic. I kept the 14 military Humvees that I was responsible for in great shape.

I pressed Kogan, "Seriously, who in the civilian world needs my service outside of Arnold Schwarzenegger who actually owns a Hummer H1?" Kogan didn't back down in the face of my excuses. He kept pushing and then made a simple statement that made all the difference in the world. He said "Patrick, I don't know what it is about you, but *I believe in YOU*. You have a way of making people feel positive in a way that I've never seen." Whether he was making this up or not, it didn't matter. This was the first time someone I trusted and believed said the words, "I believe in you."

Simple situations and simple statements can be the most

profound moments of life. The words from Kogan was one of them. I didn't have a job offer or any idea about *what* I would do, but I made the difficult decision to decline re-enlistment with the US Army. I would figure it out later.

I'm not trying to get quirky, but the reality of it is that most institutions, starting with the government down and extending to our educational system, have given up on the majority of Americans. Politicians seem to think they're helping the average citizen with outcome-based education and endless entitlement programs, but they're not. These career "public servants" seem to believe that making needy citizens feel like they need and should be grateful for government help is the right thing to do but in reality they're just making them feel like they can't stand up on their own two feet. Masses of people are being pandered to for their vote and promised support programs in return. This isn't assistance – it's enablement through entitlement programs.

To my thinking, the four-letter word that starts with "F" is FREE! Entitlement programs providing an assortment of nearly perpetual free things that rob people of the dignity that comes from accomplishment. From there, self-esteem and independence are eroded, leaving hopelessness.

Entitlement is the new heroin, and our leaders are the drug dealers. As author and satirist P.J. O'Rourke once said, "We don't need term limits – we need jail."

If you're wondering whether I'm a Republican or Democrat, actually I'm usually frustrated by BOTH parties. This led me to become a registered Independent, and I have voted for Democrats and Republicans from city council seats to the oval office. I offer that to underline that I don't have any full right or full left political agenda in the subtext. I am simply sick and tired of seeing our government and educational system abuse people (yes I used that word) with the amount of power and influence that they wield. It's almost as if they have a made everyone believe there's only one formula that leads to success.

I left the Army and took a job with Bally Total Fitness while attending Santa Monica College. I eventually dropped out and became a full-time entrepreneur who had no clue what the hell he was doing. That led me to become a failure while accumulating $49,000 of debt.

It may be confusing as you may be asking where I'm going with this dialogue but hang tight, the story will make sense.

When I hit rock bottom that first time as an entrepreneur, which seems to me a requirement for anyone who ends up being extremely successful, I met someone who introduced me to the financial industry. I somehow secured a job at Morgan Stanley Dean Witter without a four-year degree, which was virtually unheard of. I used the law of numbers by faxing (yes, we used fax back in 2001) my dull resume to 100 financial firms with a cover letter that got everyone's attention. Since my resume only had hourly-job work experience from Haagen Dazz, Burger King, Bally Total Fitness and a stint in the US Army, I had to find a way to get creative. I decided to start my cover letter with the best joke that I knew. After the joke, I wrote the following words:

"If the joke made you laugh, that's exactly how my clients will feel when they do business with me. If you want an advisor on your team that will win his clients over, I'm the right guy for your firm."

I thought this method was a long shot, but in the days after faxing this resume out, I received 30 calls with half of them simply laughing because they loved the approach but told me I wasn't qualified. The other half offered me an interview, and three offered me a job. I started with Morgan Stanley Dean Witter in the Glendale, California office. My first day of work was 9/10/2001, the day before 9/11, a day none of us will ever forget. What made it even worse was Morgan Stanley had 3,600 employees headquartered in the World Trade Center.

I studied and received the required securities licenses including my Series 7, 66, 31, as well as my Life & Health license. This accumulation of licenses became, in a way, my four-year degree. It qualified me to work in the industry and, therefore, gave a 1.8 GPA kid the opportunity to do something with my life.

After a year with Morgan Stanley, I departed and joined Transamerica to focus on Life Insurance. This was a great experience, one that led me to start my financial marketing organization, PHP Agency in October 2009. We started with just one office in Northridge, California and only 66 licensed agents. Today, PHP is licensed in 49 states and has helped nearly 3,000 individuals become licensed insurance agents. Many of these people came from backgrounds similar to my own. Coincidence? No way!

There's another angle here. I was introduced to reading books when I started working at Bally (remember the 1.8 GPA? Not a lot of reading books!). I picked up my first business book and read it. That lead me to keep reading, and today I have read over 1,200 business books (entrepreneurship, management, marketing, leadership, strategy, biographies of entrepreneurs and leaders – you name it). The wonderful thing about most business books is that anyone can read them. They don't cost $400 (on top of tuition costing $40,000 or more per a year), and you can immerse yourself in any subject. You can learn from people who have been successful and have the evidence to prove it. Anyone can read and learn, and that's exactly what I did.

One of the executives at PHP Agency, Maral Keshishian is a UCLA graduate and also earned an MBA. She once asked me if I would ever consider going back to school. I explained that if I ever go back to school it would have to be the best of the best and, to me, the two names that always come to mind were Harvard and Oxford. I asked her to look into how I could go to Harvard.

Now Harvard is not the easiest school to go to regardless of the program. Obviously, I knew I would not qualify for the undergrad program nor the three-year MBA program at Harvard Business School. Not only could I never attend any three-year program due to my business schedule, but I also wanted to find a program where I could connect with other CEOs and founders who were experiencing the same challenges I was facing so we can help each other.

She told me about Harvard's three-week "OPM Program" which stands for Owner, President, and Management and carried a price tag of $40,000. If you multiply that by 144 Entrepreneurs in attendance, it sure sounds like a profitable business to me. Apparently liberal Harvard has a capitalist hiding somewhere!

The OPM Program requires that participants must run a company that does a minimum of $10,000,000 a year in revenue and be the majority owner of the company. It's a three-year program where you stay on-campus for three weeks annually and eventually become a Harvard Alumni.

I was very particular about making sure that I wasn't going to take classes that didn't have to do with what I wanted to learn. I have no time for physics or fine arts or things that have nothing to do with running my business. I wanted ONLY to study relevant business subjects. I won't lie to you, I went in not too optimistic, but it ended up being worth the time.

Now, you can see what I meant at the beginning of this chapter when I said I chose to go to school backward and it worked for me. What if I would have forced myself to go and do what society tells us to do? What would've happened if I forced myself to grind through Santa Monica City College? This is why I believe we must make some major adjustments to our current educational system so that it delivers a great usable education outcome for 100 percent of our high school freshmen instead of just the 30 percent that graduate from college.

In many ways, college has simply become an industry unto itself and a convenient way for certain political agendas to be passed on to the next generation.

In most homes, we are told to go to college by married parents, step-parents or single parents. Our relatives and friends echo this sentiment. Setting aside the professions that require college, why does the answer seem to be that everyone should go to college? Is it tradition or aspiration? Social expectations? Or something else?

Ask enough people and a diverse list of reasons from logical and emotional viewpoints begins to form. These include the following:

1. *You need college to get a good job.*

This is usually a statement talking about a job in general rather than a statement about a specific college major or line of work. While I agree about college when it comes to science or medicine, spending money on a degree while you possess a complete lack of direction is a waste of time and money (your parents' money or worse, student loan debt!).

The truth is that you don't necessarily need a college degree to excel in many professions in life. We'll examine that in detail in an upcoming chapter.

2. *It's a time to mature and figure out what you want to do. You can always change your major as a graduation (or sobriety) comes into focus.*

A delayed decision punctuated by partying and an extended

adolescence allow you time to get your act together. In fact, some schools are known simply as party schools (they know who they are). Major websites and magazines actually publish celebratory lists!

3. *My parents or friends and family said I should go but didn't explain in deep detail.*

I am concerned that too many college decisions are made as if we are robots programmed and influenced by external peer pressure. Too often we "just do it" because we accept the notion that we are *supposed to "just do it."* Peer pressure often clouds our thinking and prevents us from pro*cessing* whether we SHOULD "just do it." Legacy or entrenched thinking like this can come from a variety of places but, personally when it comes to college, I think this pressure comes mostly from these sources:

OTHER STUDENTS

Peer pressure between high school students who, if they are honest with each other, feel insecure about many things. Bragging about the college they are planning to attend is one of many ways to cover their insecurity and go "one up" on other students. Not all students are insecure, of course, but the impact on students who are insecure or just don't know what they are going to do in life is significant. Even the best of friends can influence each other without understanding the deeper impact on each other.

I wonder just how many of these students get on the treadmill and blindly head off to college without a solidified sense of direction? Did they follow the lead of their friends despite knowing in their heart that their life course may be different? Do they go from semester to semester without passion for where they are headed? How many end up with student loan debt but no clear career direction? The stats about those who graduate and take jobs unrelated to their course of study or are "underemployed" tell a sad story.

I hope that students who read this book do one thing: open a dialogue with their friends by asking "why" they have chosen a college or major and keep asking why until you are convinced the friend is committed and passionate. Any answer about choosing a college that begins with a "B" is usually trouble: beer, boobs, bongs, bikinis, boys, beach, spring break, blunts... Yes, books start with a B, but it's usually not on the list.

To wrap up this point in a serious way, if the "whys" reveal that they aren't sure, tell them "let's keep talking about this. You have gifts and need to find your passion and use them for that and only that!"

Looking back, I wish a friend had done that for me at the end of high school. If you are 18 or under and are reading this book, please be that friend for someone today.

OUR PARENTS

Peer pressure from parents is tragically legendary. Amidst the general commentary about academic achievement-driven parents are a bevy of unfortunate and often inappropriately racial stereotypes. Did you read between the lines of Tom's real-life story in the Prologue of this book? The Asian student was depressed, and his family apparently did not or could not help. Either way, it's tragic. One wonders if they were overly focused on academic achievement to the point of adding to the pressure vs. being encouraging parents. I am not condemning those particular parents, as they experienced a horrible personal tragedy.

To properly defend parents, I'll offer this: Some parents unintentionally put pressure on their children to attend college because they are merely trying to protect them from what they see as a poor decision (not going to college) that can alter their life trajectory. Parents certainly want the best for their children, and that's not a bad thing. But to be myopic about college without processing the decision with their children can lead to the peer pressure of the parental variety.

On the other hand, we all know parents who brag about their children (ever get a holiday letter that's long on bragging and short on sincerity?) and are even living a sense of personal achievement or worth *through* their children. They are seemingly trying to keep up with other families in their social circle. They are swimming against waves of self-created mental perceptions of what they believe will be a negative perception of a child who does not go to college.

THE EDUCATION INDUSTRY

Peer Pressure from the educational system itself is often overlooked. In fact, I get strange looks when I bring it up. We forget that education is a multi-billion-dollar industry driving to earn its revenue just like any other industry. Although I just used the word "industry," that's probably the wrong term. I say that because most "industries" pay taxes. Let's not forget that the multi-billion dollar endowments held by institutions of higher education carry special status that allows them not to pay taxes on the market gains or interest earned by their endowments.

The industry obviously seeks to protect and promote the argument that higher education is *always* necessary.

Outside of research institutions that are leading and driving discovery in science and medicine, most of the liberal arts colleges and way too many undergraduate business programs simply don't live in the real world. Some do, and I am not throwing the baby out with the bathwater, but the point here is clear.

Very few professors have worked in the private sector, and that's a problem unto itself. I have an issue with those who are teaching about management without having managed someone. It's easy to talk about systems to discipline employees, but it is a different thing to look someone in the eye and terminate their employment. I served in the Army and can tell you that there was a stark difference between boot camp sergeants who served in the Gulf War and led men into active combat and those who were merely teaching the disciplines of being a soldier. Experience executing a system always trumps reading about the system in a book or simply teaching principles contained in that book.

Business disciplines can be self-taught or learned outside a university from mentors with proven track records. That's a cold hard fact that business schools don't want to admit. They preach their relevancy and necessity with predictable vigor – and this directly leads to pressure from "Education Inc." Later in this book, we have included the "Drop out Hall of Fame." Many company founders and business people are on the list. There's not one cardiologist!

On that note, getting back to the sciences, when it comes to learning about the inner workings of the human heart, students can open a cadaver or hold an actual heart in their hands long before they head into an operating room and perform a procedure on a living person. There's no need to elaborate much more than that. Advanced sciences such as medicine are best learned at a research university.

Art often parodies this reality with amazing acuity. In the original Ghostbusters movie (the good one not the remake that was a colossal flop), Ray Stanz, the main character, laments that the university may cut their grant (free money) to study ghosts and paranormal behavior. He and his two research partners readily admit that they are basically living off the grant and their research is a joke. The punchline is a 30-second speech Stanz gives in a panic about living on a grant from the University versus having a real job:

"Personally, I liked the university. They gave us money and facilities; we didn't have to produce anything! You've never been out of college! You don't know what it's like out there! I've worked in the private sector. They expect results!"

Stanz is correct. The private sector expects results and customers respond (or not) with brutal efficiency. While I feel like an entire book could be written about peer pressure, I think my point about fellow students, our parents, and the educational system itself has been made fairly well. Let's go to the next reason I hear too often about why we should go to college.

4. *You will network and meet friends that you will have for life and make contacts with the Alumni Association that will help you in your career.*

If you need to go to college to make friends or useful life contacts in a world equipped with LinkedIn and Facebook, there's something very wrong. Before connected technology and the myriad social media sites, college did present a platform that acted as a hub from which new relationships are formed. These relationships are spawned in individual classes, fraternity and sorority memberships, campus clubs and, yes, alumni associations. Today relationships are still formed this way. But to say that's a reason to spend a ton of money on college is wrong-headed and myopic.

Let's pick an overly simple example. Suppose a woman wants to be the founder of her own company. She can join groups on LinkedIn, follow founders on Twitter and use both to actually start an active, personal dialogue. If she is persistent, she may get a detailed email with advice or, better yet, a 30-minute phone call from a CEO / founder who is impressed with her persistence and zeal for knowledge.

Now let's bring her to life. It's June 2016 and Juliana from Germany is going to visit the USA. She sends a thoughtful email about wanting to learn through being a free intern while she is in the US. Her logic is this: She's already flying across the Atlantic Ocean to the East coast, so a couple more hours to Dallas is not a big deal. That's exactly what she did. She arrived at my office with nerve and enthusiasm. She stands in the lobby and boldly said, "I have watched your videos, and I simply wanted to learn in person. I am ready to be an intern for two weeks for free."

See? In the modern world of LinkedIn and social media, you don't need the alumni association to meet someone. This reason, in my estimation, is one of the weakest reason to go to college although it's one that remains well-propagated today.

This chapter is not intended to be an exhaustive list of why we go to college. It is, however, intended to begin a thought process and dialogue about WHY we go and WHO goes in the first place. I hope we have succeeded.

2

WHO SHOULD GO TO COLLEGE?

Some Should – But Many Shouldn't

*"The best part of every man's education is
that which he gives to himself."*

– Sir Walter Scott

Now that I have upset a few people with Chapter 1 and the discussion of why I believe we go to college, I'd like to answer the question of *who should go to college*, or if you are already in college, *who should stay in college?*

By now you know that I have a strong bias toward encouraging people without a clear sense of direction to NOT spend their parents' money or go into debt while meandering through college. My position on the sciences is also quite clear. Therefore, it should be no surprise that my list of people who should go to college or stay in college starts with professionals.

PATRICK BET-DAVID with THOMAS N. ELLSWORTH

PROFESSIONALS

Advanced training is required in many professions such as sciences and medicine, and college is a requirement. Doctors of whatever specialty are on the list and engineers are obviously in this category. As I mentioned in the introduction, high-end sciences are BEST learned at a college where labs and resources are available to teach and hone necessary skills. There is no replacement for teaching the depth and intricacies of STEM careers.

Microsoft founder Bill Gates wrote in his blog in 2016, "I was struck by what an amazing time it is to be a student at an institution like Caltech. In every field—from engineering and biology to chemistry and computer science—I learned about phenomenal research underway to improve our health, find new energy sources, and make the world a better place."

Many of tomorrow's innovations start today in STEM degrees. The same cannot be said for those studying world literature or Renaissance art. And, to be blunt, I feel that it is a waste of time to have STEM students forced to take liberal arts classes as part of undergraduate programs. English and writing – YES! French literature – NO!

Now let's examine the other people who should go to college – and some of this may come across as somewhat controversial.

ATHLETIC SCHOLARSHIPS

A scholarship eliminates one of the two statistically largest reasons that students drop out of college; financial stress. The other reason is inadequate academic performance. While an athletic scholarship will not ensure or address academic performance, it will certainly ensure that there will not be a mountain of student loan debt following the student home from graduation.

If you are fortunate enough to receive an athletic scholarship – take it even if you are unsure of your field of study. Regarding the topic of "big sports" scholarships (football and basketball) and how those athletes often never see a classroom, for this discussion, let's set those aside. Entire books have been written about the exploitation of student-athletes in those sports in the name of big money college sports programs. Millions are made from the images and performance of these students – yet another broken college issue. March Madness is beloved by many but what's not beloved is the class time missed by the players. That's madness!

If, however, you receive a swimming, tennis or golf scholarship, you have a wonderful opportunity to choose a field of study and get a college education for free. I am definitely biased toward athletes choosing a science or engineering field if that is their passion, of course. I am not for athletes "performing" for colleges and receiving no education in the form of ridiculous collections of courses designed for athletes who do not invest (or have time to invest due to team practices and travel schedules) in their education. That's why I mentioned football and basketball.

LAZY PEOPLE

Wait. I'm about to suggest that lazy people spend money on college. Honestly, if you have no work ethic, stay in school and learn to put in the work required to finish each class and get solid grades. I believe community college would be a good place to continue the maturing process and break free from the habits or mindset that is driving your lazy behavior. Also, some community colleges have certificate programs that take less time and are very focused on a particular topic or skill. Hopefully, you learn a skill while also learning to focus on completing what you start and break free from laziness.

There are other options different from the community college degree that offer similar outcomes including certifications through companies like Microsoft. As an example, an editor I know son got his CompTIA A+ certification. He prepped for it by watching videos, and then took the test (cost $205), and he's now built custom-made computers for people.

In any case, the best avenue for lazy people is first an objective, unclouded self-appraisal. This should be followed by intentional association with friends who are *not* lazy or procrastinators. They can help hold you accountable while you get your head together without the risk of screwing up an entrepreneurial project or losing a job.

PEOPLE WHO KNOW EXACTLY WHAT THEY WANT IN LIFE

I remember being in school and seeing kids who knew what

they were going to do in life by 9th grade. The only thing I knew that I wanted to do after high school was to chase skirts for as long as I could. I had my priorities in the right place:

1. Research how to improve my game of chasing skirts.

2. Research how I could enhance my weight-lifting routine to get bigger and stronger.

3. Research the best night clubs that I hadn't been to yet.

The good news is, I was doing a lot of research, but the bad news is that it was maybe not the best type of research.

Needless to say, I didn't have a clear set of expectations of what I should do after high school. High school went by very quickly. My mother was way too concerned about me not ending up in prison or getting myself killed. My father wanted me to find a job I liked and work hard. Although my mother did get her four-year degree in Iran in business, my father dropped out of 8th grade to help support his family.

You may come from a family of pastors where you plan on going to theology school to become a pastor one day. You may have a father who was an officer in the military, and you want to follow his footsteps by getting a degree so you can become an officer. You may have a family involved in the arts such as music, dance or acting and you want to go to the best institute to enhance your creative gifts. You may have a family who's involved in politics, and your plans are to become a lawyer so one day you can also be involved in public service. Regardless of what it is, if you are fairly clear of what you want to do as a career, then stay in school. Guess what? People who know what they want to do usually find a way to get it done.

PEOPLE WITH A HABIT OF NOT FINISHING THINGS

Be honest with yourself – do you have the habit of not finishing things? Frankly, this may be related to laziness, and the same rationale applies. Moving on from high school to a community college affords you the opportunity to enter a new environment and "find yourself" as you finish maturing into adulthood. This is not something to be ashamed of because your upbringing and other factors may be why you find yourself with this habit. It is something, however, to refuse to accept and something you *continue* to allow to happen. A little self-awareness coupled with a desire to set aside bad habits and limiting beliefs can be practiced in college where the structured atmosphere can help you develop alternative skills and habits.

Stepping back for a moment, it bears acknowledging that the debate about going to college or not and about the benefit of college has been around for a while. It also comes and goes in popular movies. Billy Madison said: *stay here as long as you can, for the love of God.* The obvious implication is that college is an escape from the realities and responsibilities of life.

I joined the chorus of debate in a video that appears on my website. I also developed an accompanying quiz that can be found at the link below:

http://www.patrickbetdavid.com/stay-school-drop-college/

It might be an interesting exercise to bookmark this page, go take the quiz before continuing to Chapter 3.

Send me a message on Snapchat (betdavid19) after taking the quiz and let me know what you got out of it. I am continually amazed at the self-reflection caused by a simple online quiz!

PATRICK BET-DAVID with THOMAS N. ELLSWORTH

3

WHO SHOULD NOT GO TO COLLEGE?

The answer is "No College" more often than you think

"Some people get an education without going to college.
The rest get it after they get out."

— Mark Twain

This is going to be a controversial chapter as I examine the question of "Who should think twice -or- drop out and why?" This is highly subjective as well, obviously slanted toward my personal experience.

The angle from which I approach this chapter is this: even though I believe that people who lack direction and initiative (lazy, etc.) *should* go to college and apply themselves in order to be ready for the realities of life, I also strongly believe that people who are *not* interested in engineering, sciences or medicine may find a faster path to their vision without college. Yes, that's controversial, but the Addendum lists a veritable hall of fame of college drop outs who changed the world.

I was invited to speak at Texas A&M to their Entrepreneurship Society program where students aspire to one day become an entrepreneur. One of the students at the end of the talk approached me in tears asking me how to break it to his parents that he hates school and wants to become an entrepreneur. I truly felt for him.

There are too many good kids that are afraid of having such a conversation with their parents or don't know where or how to start one. A big part of why I was inspired to write this book is to help parents and students start a meaningful dialogue. I think parents often are so concerned with protecting their kids from certain pains that they experienced that they actually prevent them from maximizing their potential.

Ironically, a few months after the talk at Texas A&M, on the eve of publishing this book, a national news story broke about a student who found a way to break the news to his friends, family and the rest of the world that he was dropping out. The (ex-)student is Billy Willson, a freshman at Kansas State University and he chose Facebook.

Billy is from Olathe, Kansas a suburb of Kansas City in the Midwest US where sensible values and work ethic have been the norm for generations. He is an excellent student who claimed a 4.0-grade point average.

He chose to post a controversial message on Facebook at the end of finals. He included a picture of himself "flipping off" the K-State sign and said he was dropping out immediately to follow entrepreneurial pursuits. The message must have resonated because the post immediately garnered tens-of-thousands of shares, views, and comments (supporters and critics), not to mention national news media coverage from BBC, USA Today and Huffington Post.

As the story unfolded, Billy mentioned something that energized me tremendously. He indicated that a video I posted on my Valuetainment channel on YouTube was part of his inspiration. That video was "Stay in School or Drop Out of College?" The core points in that video would become the outline for this book, and before it was even published, Billy Willson was already inspired to action.

"YOU ARE BEING SCAMMED," he declared in the Facebook post. "You may not see it today or tomorrow, but you will see it someday. Heck, you may have already seen it if you've been through college. You are being put thousands into debt to learn things you will never even use. You end up wasting 4 years of your life to be stuck at a paycheck that grows slower than the rate of inflation."

In an interview with the USA Today newspaper, he added, "I purposely made the post controversial because I knew it would help it spread so much farther. My goal with getting it to go viral is to reach out to those students who feel like they don't have a choice, and to encourage those in similar situations like me to reach their goals and feel comforted in the fact they have someone to relate to."

Will every college drop out like Billy Willson succeed? Of course not, but the obvious corollary is that everyone who fails to try when their gut says "TRY!" will almost certainly regret not trying. On the other hand, it certainly bears mentioning the obvious: a college degree does NOT assure anyone of success. There have been hundreds of articles written in the past 10 years about college graduates that are "underemployed" – having jobs that have nothing to do with their college degree.

STRONG WORK ETHIC BUT NOT CLEAR

If you have a strong work ethic and have a sense of direction (see also: Bill Gates), college may not be a place to refine your understanding or direction. Instead, it may be a place where you may delay becoming a successful entrepreneur. The list of successful entrepreneurs who dropped out to start their own businesses is long and legendary.

OBSESSIVE PERSONALITY

This may sound strange, but entrepreneurs are not perfect people. They have their quirks and ADHD, OCD and other moderate psychosis are fairly common among them. I remember being 14-years-old and obsessed with spending my time after school with role-playing games. What made RPG games addicting was that the players assume the roles of characters in a fictional setting. Most games are hero-fantasies where you have the opportunity to save the world, get the enemy and solve a problem. Two games got me addicted – Festers Quest and Final Fantasy. It was 1994 when Final Fantasy was introduced, and you couldn't stop me from playing. It was extremely difficult, and no one could finish the game. That was a challenge to me. It was almost as if I was on a mission to save the world. After many long nights and wasted hours, I eventually finished Festers Quest and Final Fantasy. The strangest thing about video games is that I lost all interest in them right after high school, which was a good thing. I have known men in their 20s, and 30s who waste evenings addicted to Grand Theft Auto or Call of Duty.

The point I'm making is that the same level of obsession, and even ADHD or OCD, that drives a teenager to stay up all night for months on end until they "finish" a game is the same obsessive commitment it will take to start a company and produce the next innovative product for the world.

FULLY UNDECIDED

Why waste your parents' money or go into debt needlessly? A short stint at a local two-year community college may be a better choice. Such an option would allow you to live at home and discover your passion. There's no sin in being undecided, but it seems foolish to spend big money on a four-year college if you are entirely undecided. Further to the point, the first two years of college are comprised mostly of general education courses. So it goes, why not complete those at a community college and save the money?

GREAT IN SALES

If you excel in sales and already know that this is the line of work for you, you may consider skipping college. The list of self-made people in pharmaceutical, real estate, insurance, online stores, mortgages and other professional services is long and distinguished. Assuming sales is your passion, seriously consider passing on college to hone your skills. Any number of companies offer compelling training programs for promising sales people. There are also a litany of professional sales skills courses available online where you can hone your skills at home in the evening without the time and cost associated with attending these same seminars in the past.

The website Skilledup (www.skilledup.com) had some interesting thoughts on sales for college graduates, but I say these are equally applicable for those NOT headed to a four-year university:

"[Some people] may turn your nose up at the very idea of taking a job in sales. You may consider it a step-down, or maybe beneath your qualification and I get where you're coming from, but that's looking at it in completely the wrong way. I'm not saying you should look into a career in sales (although that is an excellent choice), just that you should look at taking a job in sales for the time being.

Do you consider yourself overqualified for sales? Instead of thinking that's a bad thing, think of it as an advantage. The low barrier to entry should make it all the more easy for you to get hired. "But why would I want to get hired in sales in the first place?" you ask. Because working in sales will teach you valuable transferable skills, pad your resume, and above all pad your wallet with unlimited income potential.[ii]

I could not agree more! A career in sales can be one of the more lucrative careers for those with the core aptitudes for such a career.

A BIT REBELLIOUS

I remember going to Sunday school in Iran at six years old and questioning every single thing my Sunday school teacher said. The poor lady couldn't handle me, so she finally asked me to leave the class. She told my father that I questioned every single part of the Bible. I wasn't trying to be smart-alecky, I simply was curious why a God who loves people would allow Iraq to bomb us the way they did. It just didn't make any sense to me, so I questioned God. I was always categorized as a kid that was rebellious and didn't do well with authority. It got me into trouble many times in my life, but eventually, I had to learn to shift from being a rebel without a cause to a rebel with a worthy cause. That's what changed everything.

So if you're someone who is finding yourself in the detention room or constantly meeting with the principal, you first need to adjust and stay out of life-altering trouble, but there may also be something good in there that most people – maybe even you - can't yet see.

SELF-DISCIPLINED AND COMPETITIVE

You can always tell when someone is extremely competitive. Ever since my oldest son, Patrick could speak, he always wanted to let me know that he can do everything better than me. He would say, "Daddy, one day I'm going to be bigger than you" Or "Daddy; I put my clothes on so fast today." There's something inside of a competitor that always thinks about ways of doing something better, bigger or faster.

These are often the drivers that lead an entrepreneur to start a business. Jeff Bezos thought he could do it better, bigger and faster than Borders and Barnes & Noble, which he did – and then took Amazon far beyond books. Elon Musk believed he could create an online payment system and do it sooner, better and faster than traditional banks, which he did. The one thing both have in common is that they are extremely competitive.

Self-disciplined and competitive people with a mind to launch an entrepreneurial project can rely on those character traits to get them through the tough initial days of any new venture. These individuals may feel bored or constrained by college as well. Interestingly, Amy Rosen a partner at the Public Private Strategy Group (PPSG) penned an article in February 2016 titled *"Colleges Face Challenges in the Entrepreneur Arms Race."* In that article, she examined the disconnect between entrepreneurial spirit and the typically regimented college curriculum, "The challenge (faced by colleges) is that many of the characteristics that make entrepreneurs successful are **the very things that make traditional college learning environments challenging for them**. Creative and out of the box thinking, as well as finicky temperaments, have been shown to be shared characteristics of many successful entrepreneurs can be liabilities in college. Said another way, the qualities that make good students don't always translate well to entrepreneurship. Many round entrepreneur pegs are out of place in square-holed schools. That's not news. Thomas Edison, perhaps the nation's foremost innovator, and entrepreneur didn't finish school. And that connection hasn't abated."[iii]

Interesting isn't it? The educational industry is keenly aware of entrepreneurs and is trying to react and sell them an education.

GOOD AT MAKING FRIENDS

Being good at making friends is not the same as having a large number of friends. You may be a star athlete at your high school and attract "friends," but this is not the same as making friends. Those who have the ability to make friends may possess charisma or have learned the art of establishing and maintaining a connection with people on a personal level. These connections may be profound and enduring, or they may be transactional – such as getting to know the security guy at a local club so you can get in when the line is long.

This skill is a core competency that many salespeople have mastered. As you read this book, you will see how I (and others) feel about sales and its applicability to many career vectors as well as a lucrative career in sales itself.

Someone who can make friends easily may be a better networker and may find it easier to build relationships that pay off either now or down the road. When I see someone that makes friends easily and that someone is likable, I know that person can go a long way in business. People are drawn to individuals who make friends easily.

HAVE A MENTOR

In Chapter 5, I explain that offering to work for a CEO for free is a bold way to learn. If you have a mentor, particularly a CEO / founder of a successful company, take the opportunity to learn from them. I believe such an opportunity is worth more than a Harvard MBA. In Chapter 6 I reference Mark McCormack's book,

What They Don't Teach you at Harvard Business School. Mark was the founder of IMG the sports agency that pioneered so many of the things we take for granted in professional tennis and golf. Can you imagine what you could have learned from Mark?

The above reasons comprise my own list, and it is not presented for your consideration without rational analysis. There are other lists out there circulating which say some very similar things. In March 2016 Sienna Beard wrote the article *"5 Reasons Why You Shouldn't Go to College."* [iv] In that piece, she presented her own list, and I have included much of it here:

---

1. You need to work now

While many students hold a part-time job while they are in school, and some work full time, this path can be very demanding. It can be especially difficult to juggle a full-time job and a full-time course load. A 2013 New City and Seventeen magazine survey found that nearly four out of five (almost 80 percent) are working while going to school.

2. The potential loans are overwhelming

College is expensive. While loans are often an expected part of the college experience, not everyone wants to take out a loan. It's important to remember that when you finish college, you will have to pay the loans back with interest, and it's possible that your job will not pay as well as you hope, or that you may not find a job immediately. College students are working while attending school.

3. You don't know what you want to do with your life

Many high school students go to college because it's expected of them, but that isn't a good reason to go. If you are facing peer pressure from your parents, friends, or teachers to attend college, but you don't feel ready, then now is not the time to go. You shouldn't take on such a large financial and time commitment just to please other people. This is especially true if you don't know what you want to do with your life. College is expensive, and it doesn't make sense to spend money on a college degree if you are unsure of your path. You also risk taking extra time to finish your degree if you switch your major multiple times. You are better off waiting to attend college when you know what you want to do with your life.

4. You don't need a degree

Several jobs pay well without a degree. The specific job requirements will depend on the company, but according to University.com, Web Developers and Network and Computer Systems Administrators are two examples. There are also several careers that pay well but only require an associate's degree or certificate. If you don't need a college degree to do what you love (or to bring in more money), then you shouldn't enroll in classes. Many people find that they have a specific skill that translates well into a career without requiring a college degree. Others simply start at the bottom of a company and work their way up, and others join a family business and learn the ropes without going to college.

5. You're not prepared academically

If you blew off most of high school, or you simply had a difficult time understanding various subjects, then college might not be the right choice for you. If you attend college and you end up failing multiple classes, you will only be wasting money. Community college is a great idea for many people and for many reasons, and if you had a hard time in high school, but you are ready to take your education seriously, then community college can be a great place to start.

I appreciate Sienna Beard's approach to her list and can see elements inside her list that harmonize with my list. Combine them, and you have a solid list of rationale to consider as you process the question.

There's another voice that I found very compelling. In 2013 Ryan Holiday, author (*Trust Me, I'm Lying*, and *The Obstacle is The Way*) and visionary marketer, wrote a blog entitled *"How Dropping Out Of College Can Save Your Life"* that became the #1 Google result for the search term "dropping out of college." Here is that blog post:

"One has to kill a few of one's natural selves to let the rest grow - a very painful slaughter of innocents." – Henry Sidgwick.

You, the ambitious young person, how many of your natural selves have you identified yet? How many of them are suffocating? Are you prepared for the collateral damage that's going to come along with letting the best version of you out?

My victims:

Ryan, college student 1 year from graduating with honors

Ryan, the Hollywood executive, and wunderkind

Ryan, director of marketing for American Apparel

All dead before 25. May they rest in pieces.

I am a perpetual dropout, quitting, abandoning or changing paths just as many others in my position would be getting comfortable. By Sidgwick's terms, I guess I am a serial killer. This "slaughter" made room for the exponential growth of Ryan Holiday, published author. But he better not get comfortable either. Because he too may have to be killed one day. And that will be a good thing.

Because the future belongs to those who have the guts to pull the trigger. Who can drop out and fend for themselves? If you're reading this site, you might already be contemplating a decision like that. I want to show you why it might be the right call for you and how to do it.

The Big Myth

"It wasn't quite a choice, it was a realization. I was 28, and I had a job as a market researcher. One day I told my psychiatrist that what I really wanted to do was quit my job and just write poetry. And the psychiatrist said, 'Why not?' And I said, 'What would the American Psychoanalytic Association say?' And he said, 'There's no party line.'" – Allen Ginsberg

Let's get the big myth out of the way. There's not much dropping involved in dropping out of school. When I did it, I remember walking to the registrar's office — I was so nervous. My parents had disowned me, I needed to move to a new city, the girl whose job I stole hated me. Why was I doing it? I'd just helped sign my first multi-platinum rock act, and I wasn't about to go back to the dorms and tolerate reading in the newspaper about other people doing my work. I was 20 years old.

I'm here to drop out of school, I announced to the registrar (like I was some presidential candidate who thinks he literally has to throw his hat into a ring). In fact, as my advisor informed me, that wasn't exactly necessary. I could take a leave of absence for up to a year and possibly more, without even jeopardizing my scholarship. I braced for the same condescending, paternalistic lecture I'd gotten from my parents. It didn't come. These people were happy for me. And if I submitted the right forms, I might even be able to get course credit for the work. How's that for a party line?

So I took the plunge, and like many big risks, it turned out that dropping out of school was more manageable than I could have ever anticipated.

What I Wish I'd Known

I get a lot of emails from kids who are on the verge of dropping out. They always seem so scared. And I empathize with them. I know I was scared when I quit. Even billionaires, years removed from the decision that has now, in their case, been clearly vindicated, still speak of the hesitation they felt when they left school. Were they doing the right thing? What would happen? Were they throwing everything away?

It's the scariest and most important decision most young entrepreneurs, writers, artists will ever make. So naturally, they take it very seriously. But doing that — taking it so seriously — almost wrecked me.

I remember pulling into a parking space one day a few months after dropping out, stressed and on the verge of a breakdown. Why am I killing myself over this?, I thought. It's just life. Suddenly, a wave of calm washed over me. I was doing what young people are supposed to do: take risks. There is no need to stress over anything so seriously, let alone school (as someone told me later, he'd gotten sick when he was in college and missed 18 months of school. He's 50 now and a year and a half seems like two seconds). I'm not going to starve. I'm not going to die. There is nothing that can't be undone. Just relax. Relax. And I did. And it worked.

If I'd realized it sooner, I could have avoided many needlessly sleepless nights.

I also wish someone had given me some more practical advice:

Try to have a few months of money on hand. This makes you feel less financial pressure and gives you more power negotiating because you can say "No!".

Keep a strong network of friends — college friends especially. The unusualness of your situation is a warping force.

Keep connected to normal people so you can stay grounded.

Take notes! I wish I'd written down my observations and lessons for myself the first time I dropped because it wasn't my last time and I could have prepared better for round II and III.

Why I Did It Again (and again)

When I dropped out of school, I was betting on myself. It was a good bet (one that surprised me, honestly). In less than 3 years, I'd worked as a Hollywood executive, researched for and promoted multiple NYT bestsellers, and was Director of Marketing for one of the most provocative companies on the planet. I had achieved more than I ever could have dreamed of — the scared, overwhelmed me of 19 could have never conceived of having done all that. (Which is why I killed that younger version of me). Yet, I knew it was time to drop out again. The six-figure job had to go. It was time for the next phase of my life. What I had, just like college had been, was holding me back.

That's what I did. I left and moved 2,000 miles away to write a book. It was wracking and risky and hard for everyone in my life to understand. But I was prepared this time. I knew what to expect. I'd saved my money, I built up my support system, and I refused to take it too seriously. Whatever happened, I probably wouldn't die.

…and I didn't. In fact, within six months I'd sold the book to Penguin for several times my previous salary and was securely on my new path.

Welcome to the Future

The many people who email me and I seem to have a funny habit: We repeatedly leave and give up the things that most people work so hard to achieve. Good schools. Scholarships. Traditional jobs. Money. We don't believe in sunk costs. If that sounds like you, then you're probably a perpetual drop out too. Embrace it. I have.

I know that I will do it again and again in my life. Why? Because every time I do, things get better. The trial by fire works. It's the future. The institutions we have built to prop us up seem mostly to hold creative and forward thinking people back. College is great, but it is slow and routine. Corporations can do great things, but fulfilling individuals is not one of them. Money is important, but it can also be an addiction. Accomplishments like a degree or a job are not an end; they are a means to an end. I'm so glad I learned that.

On your own path in life, remember the wise words of Napoleon and "Trade space for time." (Or if you prefer the lyrics of Spoon "You will never back up an inch ever/that's why you will not survive.") Space is recoverable. The status of a college degree, the income from a job — recoverable. Time is not. This time you have now is it. You will not get it back. If you are stuck in a dorm room or wedged into a cubicle but what you are doing outside of those places is the greatest possible use of you, then it's time to drop out.

Acknowledge, as Marcus Aurelius writes, the power inside you and learn to worship it sincerely. It may seem counter-intuitive that dropping out — quitting — is part of that, but it is. It's faith in yourself. It's about not needing a piece of paper or other people's validation to know you have what it takes and are worth betting on. This is your life; I hope you take control and get everything you can out of it.

———————————

Wow! Is that thought-provoking or what? I deeply appreciate Ryan's approach to processing the question! If you don't have his books on your shelf, you are missing some of the best self-introspective writing.

In determining whether to go to college or not, an important factor can be not to confuse the passion with the profession. For example, someone who loves to teach doesn't necessarily need to be a teacher in the conventional sense. They can create online courses. There are ways to exercise a gift or calling without going the traditional route.

Another example is someone may want to be a counselor because people go to them with their problems, and they like helping people. But they can still use that gift in other ways, such as being a mentor, coach, etc. and for those options, college isn't necessary.

As you identify your passion, look for ways to use and apply that gift in a manner that does not require a college degree.

4

THE BUSINESS OF COLLEGE

Students or Customers?

There Are Things People Aren't Talking About

"I turned down a scholarship to Yale. The problem with college is that there's a tendency to mistake preparation for productivity. You can prepare all you want, but if you never roll the dice, you'll never be successful."

\-   Shia LaBeouf

"Over 40 percent of full-time four-year college students fail to earn a bachelor's degree within six years, and many never complete their education." That dim news was boldly reported in "Working Paper 109" Published by the highly-respected Calder Research Partners.   Further, the Calder report went on to say that many students were likely dropouts and should have attended a two-year college (community college) before matriculating to a larger university.

Let's unpack that bit from the Calder report: colleges are accepting students who they know are going to drop out.   While this keeps the tuition revenue machine humming during freshman-sophomore years, the human cost from that point forward is horrifying.

In March of 2016, Fortune Magazine writer Sheila Blair reported on the dropout epidemic and discussed the issue of "student retention." She also exposed the shameless President of Mount Saint Mary's College who worried more about the institution's rankings (and the ability to attract new students) than he did about the fate of currently enrolled students.[vi]

Blair's article said, "For instance, take the issue of retention. A cold business analysis would support the direct solution Mount St. Mary's President apparently wanted to pursue – kick them out before they can hurt the schools' rankings. Someone with an academic orientation might see the retention problem a little differently – a failure of admissions policies to identify students who can succeed and/or insufficient support services for students once admitted."

Blair summed it up perfectly. In Chapter 1 I noted that pressure to attend college comes, in part, from the educational industry itself. Do you see any difference between the President of Mount Saint Mary's College and the General Motors CEO who was hauled off to testify at a congressional hearing because GM allegedly did nothing to protect consumers who were buying GM cars with faulty ignition switches? To me, there's no difference. GM and Mount Saint Mary's took the customer's money and did little to nothing to protect them.

If you look at rising costs, the indictment grows longer. Over the 10 years starting in 2005 and ending in 2014 statistics clearly show the same number of students is enrolled in college over that time but today's the costs have risen tremendously:

College Enrollment 0 percent growth (unchanged)

Tuition: Up 54 percent

Student Debt: Up 157 percent

(Source: Federal Reserve Board; National Center for Education Statistics)

Is it any wonder financial stress and academic performance are the two overwhelming reasons why students drop out?

Some of this was further reiterated by CNBC - John Schoen did a great job in the segment "Why college costs are so high and rising."

A 45-year-old person is in the prime of their career. By that time, people have amassed high-level expertise at whatever they do. Still, a lot has changed since our 45-year old example was born in 1971. Let's take a look at how things have changed since they entered the world by reflecting on the numbers presented by Schoen and CNBC.

Here's the chart:

Economic Indicator	1971	Today
Housing – Average Home Price	$23,900	$281,500 11X
Public University – Tuition	$500	$9,139 18X
Private College – Tuition	$1,831	$31,231 17X

That's a startling analysis. The cost of getting yourself educated in America has risen 18X. This is an incredible rate of change, and it certainly explains the student loan crisis in America today.

Any normal person would likely assume that wages have risen to keep up with the cost of education. The shocking truth is no; it has not. Let's take a look at wages over that same period:

Economic Indicator	1971	Today
Personal Income	$10,600	$53,657 5X

WAIT - WHAT?!?!?

Wages have risen 5X while the annual tuition cost of public university or private college has risen from 17X to 18X!

The blunt conclusion is the average family in America cannot afford to put their children through college. How then did their children get through college? The answer is simple yet tragic: someone went into debt at staggering levels. Usually, it's their

68

children – the students.

Paying off the debt is another matter entirely. Let's do some very basic math:

Public University: $9,139 X 4 years = $36,556

Private College: $31,231 X 4 years = $124,924

Assuming a college degree earns an above-average income of $60,000 and assuming that individual can somehow manage to live and apply 10 percent of their gross income to pay off the debt, it will still take over six years to pay off a public university and an astounding 21 years to pay off a private college. Obviously, their income will rise over that time, but the point stands – the cost is becoming prohibitive for the average family, and the indebtedness of the graduating student is staggering.

In late 2014 nearly all the news networks covered the announcement that student loan debt in the US had eclipsed consumer credit card debt. Let me say that again; students who had graduated college had MORE collective debt than the credit card debt held by rest of the nation which, ahem, included their parents sitting in the audience and cheering as they received their diploma!

It was absolutely shocking to me that despite broad and accurate media coverage there was not the same level of visceral outrage over student debt that there had been for consumer credit card debt and home loan defaults only six years earlier.

Finally, in the 2016 election, college debt came up and caught the attention it deserves, although the solution was not feasible. Bernie Sanders, a Senator from Vermont, made the argument that public colleges should be free. He claimed by taxing certain Wall Street transactions. Wait – every problem can't be solved by "tax the rich." If we start giving everything for free what's the limit? That's a whole other problem, so let's stay with student loan debt.

How's it possible that a nearly unknown Senator from Vermont was able to get 11 million Americans to donate to his campaign and if it weren't for the super delegates which are a key part of the American presidential nomination system, he would've beaten Hillary Clinton and been the Democratic candidate for President. The point isn't whether you liked Clinton, Trump or Sanders, the real question to ask is what caused this enthusiasm about Bernie. Students and adults around the country started thinking about why we have so much college debt. Bernie questioned it, and it made America start asking important questions, and that is a very good thing.

I believe this is a subject that keeps getting put aside because of its complexity, but there are darker sides to student loan debt involving the government. For example, the concept of student loans was to ensure America had a supply of educated workers to drive the economy and pay taxes which keep the country running. But as it evolved, the government ended up making lucrative profits on student loans. Today, the interest rates on student loans are currently higher than basic 30-year mortgages which are insured by a different branch of the same federal government handling the student loans. One of Bernie's campaign thrusts was exposing that over the next decade (2016-2025) the federal government will make a profit of $110 Billion on student loans. No wonder people reacted so strongly to Bernie!

When the "Great Recession" of 2007-2009 hit the US economy, banking and financial CEOs were pillaged in the press. Some of them were crooks who deserved the harsh criticism that was levied upon them. Others simply followed their industry on the path to ruin.

Sub-prime loans, credit card interest rates, a lack of qualification standards and other facts led to a financial bubble in real estate that caught some unwary or unsophisticated consumers by surprise. Other consumers knew what they were doing and deserved their financial fate.

The heat generated in the media over the great recession was an all-consuming fire that stayed in the headlines for nearly two years. The student loan debt story garnered media, but it pretty much came and went in the news cycle.

In the classic comedy, *Animal House*, "Flounder" the nickname of a simple-minded but good-hearted student, naively allows his fraternity to take his brothers' brand new Lincoln on a joyride. The car is severely damaged causing Flounder to look at the wrecked Lincoln and break down in tears. Without an ounce of remorse, an elder frat brother puts an arm around the sobbing Flounder and

PATRICK BET-DAVID with THOMAS N. ELLSWORTH

says, "You screwed up – you trusted us." I feel like millions of students and graduates are looking at the wreckage of their student loan debt while their college or university is unapologetic and the government is demanding payments. In effect they are saying "You screwed up – you trusted us." Some may take offense at that reference, but I honestly don't know if there is a way to make the point without strong language.

In an even more ironic move, these same universities have sophisticated "Development" departments comprised of professional fundraising executives who have a simple mission: chase-down successful alumni and make impoverished pleas for their support to keep the beloved alma matter "relevant for the next generation." Thanks to Google, we can easily find the endowment level of just about any college in the US. Universities are sitting on multi-billion dollar endowments while they send slick pitches to beg for more from their graduates – who emerged in debt and in search of jobs. I just proffered a rather sweeping generalization, and clearly, not all universities have such endowments. The larger ones do, however, and they are often the lead offenders when it comes to funding the more sophisticated alumni pursuit programs (a.k.a. ballroom chicken dinner shakedowns).

Where does the discussion go from here? I think it's simple: we should encourage a fair percent of the nation's high school graduates who are NOT considering engineering, science, and medicine to think twice about romping directly into a college. Not only will it potentially avoid student debt and an avoidable dropout statistic, but there may also be other ways to become educated and succeed in life.

When you consider what has happened in the past 10 years, the conclusion is that America doesn't need health care reform as much as it needs educational reform. The system is broken in many respects and its harder than ever for families and students to afford a formal education. Looking through that lens, is it any wonder that the gap between the top 10 percent of society and the other 90 percent has become so much wider?

Sometimes I wonder why so many university professors love sharing ideas right out of the Communist Manifesto while bashing capitalism as an evil economic system. I speak to many young students who share stories about how their professor couldn't help themselves and relentlessly bashed capitalism. How's that possible when you represent an institution that does everything in a capitalist way and what's ever more embarrassing is that they do it at the cost of the most naïve generation. It's tougher to rip-off and manipulate a 40-year-old adult, but it's very easy to prey on 18-year-olds who are trying to figure themselves out. That's guilty by association if you ask me.

The increase in tuition cost isn't the only thing that's driving up the cost of higher education. Textbook prices have skyrocketed to levels we've never seen before.

According to a recent study done by NBC, this is what's

happened to the cost of textbooks. *"Since 2006, the cost of a college textbook has increased by 73 percent — or more than four times the rate of inflation — according to Covering the Cost, a new report from the non-profit Student PIRGs (Public Interest Research Groups). It's not uncommon for an individual book to cost more than $200, and some have price tags that go as high as $400, the report said."*[vii]

I went and got one of the textbooks that cost $200 to purchase and sent it to a good friend of mine who prints books for a living. I asked him to send me an estimate of what it would cost for me to order 5,000 copies of that same exact textbook. My goal was to figure out what the universities cost was for these books. She called me and told me that they could do it for roughly $5 a copy.

WHAT?

They're selling the book for 40 times what it costs them to make it? And they're forcing these young 18-year-olds to buy the book or else? Why isn't the media screaming at the top of their lungs about this?

Recently, there was an article written by Time about Apple Inc on how much it costs them to make the iPhone 7 and what they sell it for. This is how the headline of the article reads

"The iPhone 7 Costs You 3x More Than It Costs Apple to Make". That's quite a markup. [viii]

The market price for a 32GB iPhone 7 is $649, yet the phone reportedly

costs Apple just $225 to build.

Apple is getting criticized for selling the iPhone 7 for 3X what it cost them to make it. I would love to see Alicia Adamczyk who wrote the article to write about the institution that's making a product that only costs $5 to make and selling it for $200. Talk about a 40X markup. Media and universities are very quick to call capitalists greedy, but I think it's pretty obvious who the greedy ones are in this example. Frankly, I think educational reform would take way too long. We need air strikes.

PATRICK BET-DAVID with THOMAS N. ELLSWORTH

5

BEFORE YOU DROP OUT…

Have A Plan.
(A spontaneous reaction is NOT a plan.)

"If you don't design your own life plan,
chances are you'll fall into someone else's plan.
And guess what they have planned for you?
Not much!"

– Jim Rohn

Assuming you are in college, before you drop out of college there are a couple things to do in order to build a plan covering WHAT you will do instead of toiling in courses that are not meaningful, or you cannot understand and running up a mountain of student loan debt in the process. I have compiled a list of five possible things that you can do if you choose to drop out.

1. Have a source of support or a plan to generate an adequate source of income.

This may seem like an obvious point, but there's actually more to it than meets the eye. I am not saying get whatever job you can get and "go to work." I am saying have some source of support or figure out how to live incredibly cheaply.

2. Learn Sales

I believe this is by far the most important skill to learn in life. Whether you have plans of being the next great real estate and media mogul, and eventually become the President of United States (Wait, didn't that happen to Donald J. Trump?), or you just want to run a small restaurant in your local community, you will need to learn sales. Sales is often the separator between someone who gets the promotion and the person who doesn't. It's the separator between the guy who ends up with the prettiest girl in school and the one who doesn't. It all comes down to sales.

Whether you become an entrepreneur and are pitching investors or making a presentation to co-workers in a corporate environment, learning the art of sales is a skill that you can take with you wherever you go. Now, I do not suggest you sell used cars – the quality and application of the sales skills you learn are as important as the skills themselves. In a separate chapter, I shared a link to an article presented by Skillsup.com that validates my opinion about this issue.

3. Learn Self Discipline

The best place, in my experience and opinion, to learn self-discipline is in the military. Each branch is different, and I tend to favor the Air Force over the others even though I served in the Army. A tour in the Air Force will teach you self-discipline at a level I cannot begin to communicate. You will also travel and see different parts of the world.

4. Work under a CEO Entrepreneur for free

Assuming you have some savings or your parents are willing to support you, do whatever is necessary to contact CEOs or Presidents of businesses in your town and make a bold offer: "I'd like to work for you for six months for free." Offer to do whatever is required to make their life easier in exchange for being able to see how they process problems, run their business, deal with people and approach life in general. Refine your approach and don't give up – you WILL find one CEO who is an entrepreneur who is impressed with your grit and will agree to the deal.

Along the way, keep in mind, it doesn't necessarily have to be in town. Depending on the type of work, technology makes it possible to work for people anywhere in the world, and much learning can happen even if you aren't in the same room all the time, or ever. True, there are some advantages to face-to-face time, but the entire world is one Skype call away, and this opens up more opportunities than are available in any one geographic location.

If you are successful doing this, you will learn more in six months than you can possibly imagine. You may even turn the opportunity into a long-term, full-time job working for that CEO.

5. Start a business – launch an entrepreneurial effort.

One such individual who chose this path is Sean Kim, the founder of Rype, a foreign language training company.

Here is Sean Kim in his own words – this account has circulated online and was featured in the Huffington Post[ix].

I'm Sean Kim. It's 2014, and two years ago, I dropped out of college.

It feels like yesterday when I was unfolding my acceptance letter into McGill University in Montreal. It was the most gratifying moment of my life to have been accepted into one of the top institutions in North America.

I remember saying to myself: "This is it. I made it."

At school, I was surrounded by peers who were far smarter and more ambitious than me, and I took intriguing courses that piqued my brain's curiosity.

Every moment was a privilege.

You may now be wondering, why the hell did I drop out of school if every moment was a privilege? Let me start off by saying—it was the hardest decision I've ever made. Not just for myself, but for my family.

My mom, who was brought up in a conservative Korean background, was more excited than I was to see me hurl my graduation cap in the air for convocation. The truth is, the phrase "self-employed" is not uttered lightly among our family while dropping out of college is strictly forbidden. When I broke the news, apart from the immediate surprise, I could sense they were overwhelmingly worried about my decision.

The questions of doubts continuously piled up one after

another every time we spoke. I knew I had to back up my decision.

I spent months doing research and spoke with several career advisors and successful business leaders before I made a final decision—I had to make sure I was making the right choice.

Now I'm going to share with you what I learned through this process to help you decide if formal education is right for you.

It's Not A Safer Decision

A rising number of school graduates are realizing that they can no longer exchange their degree for a job upon graduation. The old promise made by our education system was that if you put in your time at school, you would be guaranteed a stable job as a reward for your efforts.

According to the Federal Reserve Bank of New York:

"51 percent (1.5 million) of recent graduates were either jobless or underemployed in 2013. This is up from 47 percent in 2007. Yet, the number of bachelor degree-holders has increased by 38 percent since 2000."

A degree is supposed to signal to employers and the world that you are above average. You are smart. You are hard-working. You are driven. You are worth investing in or taking a chance on. That may have been true at one time, but not anymore.

Skill Is More Important Than A Degree

Students entering college shouldn't bet on today's job market.

They should bet on the job market five to 10 years from now. And what the job market is going to require is skill—not a degree.

If we taught surfing like we prep for careers, you'd spend twenty years reading about how to surf before even touching one.

PATRICK BET-DAVID with THOMAS N. ELLSWORTH

The day you graduate, you'd be dropped out in the middle of the ocean and be told, "Good luck!"

Fortunately, learning a new skill has never been so easy or more accessible. There are plenty of places to learn skills online for free or cheap. Whether it's learning how to program, trade stocks, use Excel, design—the list goes on. Some of the top universities around the world, like Stanford University, have also opened up free online courses for anyone who wants to sign up.

The best way to prep for a career is not to sit in a lecture hall for three hours listening to something you're not truly passionate about.

It's to do it on your own.

In this economy, businesses don't have the time or capital to train you to become employable. To differentiate yourself, you have to learn in-demand skills—a framed degree doesn't get you very far anymore.

It's Who You Know That Matters!

Whether you like it or not, this is the truth: If you know the right people, you'll find the right opportunities.

As it turns out, between 60 to 80 percent of jobs are found through personal relationships. This means you should constantly be looking for more ways to expand your network—both online and offline.

Rather than trying to score that extra one percent on your accounting assignment, start attending networking events and conferences. You can find tons at Meetup.com or Eventbrite.com. This is the best and most personal way to meet people who have similar interests and goals as you. Keep in touch, help each other out and grow your community.

"We are the average of the five people we spend the most time with." —Jim Rohn

Start surrounding yourself with people who inspire you.

Dropping out isn't for everyone! This is a point I really need to emphasize.

A formal education is particularly important for those who are interested in the STEM fields (science, technology, engineering, mathematics). In these fields, not only is a bachelor's degree necessary, but that alone may not even cut it. Master's degrees and PhDs are, in many cases, expected.

And for a good reason.

You wouldn't want a surgeon to perform surgery on you, knowing he recently received a certification from an online course.

Some specialized careers will always require formal education—period.

Rather than trying to decide whether or not you need a college degree, discover your passion. See which career path fits your interests, then assess whether a college degree would be an asset to your path to success.

I'd suggest creating a list of topics or activities you enjoy indulging yourself on outside of school and work and thinking back to the classes that intrigued you most.

The point is, no one can tell you what your passions are, it's all up to you.

I studied economics and finance at McGill and, although I knew the benefits of having a strong financial background, my heart was always set on being an entrepreneur.

It didn't make financial sense to spend $20,000 and time on courses that were not significantly contributing to my long-term goal.

I'm not saying this is all easy.

The last 24 months have been the toughest times in life— emotionally and physically— from working 16 hour days, having to shut down my business, being homeless for two weeks, and working to start another one.

It's also been the most enriching and life-changing. I've learned more about myself in these 24 months than I would have in 10 years. There's nothing like looking at yourself in the mirror at your lowest moments to make you realize what you were meant to do in this life and settling for nothing less.

Throughout this experience, I've realized that if you want to make something happen, you can. The most difficult part is taking that first leap.

I had no idea what would come out of dropping out of college to pursue my dreams in the real world.

But one thing was clear.

The lessons I would learn from this experience would be far more valuable than my time spent in the lecture room. In life, there will always be an opportunity to try to get more money, cars or shoes—but the one thing you will never have more of is time.

I can now live life on my own terms, pursuing the passions that I love, and waking up every morning excited to take on new

DROP OUT AND GET SCHOOLED

challenges.

College-dropout-to-freedom

If you feel like you're stuck in school—like you're in a drought and you want something different for yourself—take my advice above and consider your options.

After weighing all your options, you still feel strongly about dropping out and feel confident that you want to do it for the right reasons, then do it.

It's scary. It's hard. But so is the status quo.

For many people in our society, the word "dropout" still leaves a bad taste in their mouths. But I want to point out one thing to keep in mind:

This article was written using a computer designed by Apple, co-founded by a college dropout: Steve Jobs. Once I'm finished, I'll save it in Microsoft Word, a software made by a company that was co-founded by Bill Gates, another dropout. Once it's published, I'll share it on Twitter, co-founded by college dropouts Jack Dorsey, Evan Williams and Biz Stone, and Facebook, co-founded by dropout Mark Zuckerberg. Everything around you was built and designed by other dropouts who couldn't stand for the status quo.

Break free and follow your passion. Learn by doing, not through a textbook. Embrace failure and do something that makes you feel excited to wake up every morning. Be different. Be unique.

This is what will matter in the end—not your degree.

Wow. Is that powerful? Sean Kim speaks from experience

about the risks – but also the rewards. If you don't go to college or you drop out, the lesson is clear – you need a plan, even if the plan is to step into the unknown.

6

WHAT SHOULD BE ADDED TO COLLEGE?

What They Don't Teach You Can Hurt You

"To be successful in life, what you need is education not literacy and degrees."

– Munshi Premchand, Indian Writer

By now you probably believe that I have a bias against college. Actually, I don't. To repeat what I have said a couple times, there are professions that require college, but there are people who would do well to think twice about running off to college with the rest of the bleating herd.

I do have a bias against many of the general education requirement courses that colleges force students to take (and pay for) on the road to earn the degree within the major that they are seeking. Tom asked a question in the Prologue to this book; "Why on Earth do they require business students to take Astronomy?" Depending on who you speak to, you will typically receive one of two answers:

(A) A college education needs to be well-rounded, and these courses provide a balance of disciplines in addition to the concentrated teaching in the major of study.

(B) Colleges make the rules and collect the tuition.

OK, so answer "B" can be seen as a bit cynical – but is it really? In the face of the staggering student debt and the load being placed on students, is it time to rethink these general education courses? I say yes!

In the book "Blue Ocean Strategy" the authors make a compelling argument. Instead of being in a shark infested ocean where all the sharks (competitors) are fighting for the same customers where they eventually end up killing each other, go create new value in a new product or market and "have a new blue ocean to yourself."

The authors presented what they call the "Four Actions Framework." Here's that diagram:

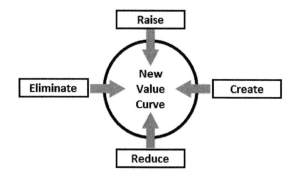

I'd like to take a crack at applying college education to the Four Actions Framework from Blue Ocean.

Create:

- Create a certain curriculum that matches the personality type of the students. Not this current dynamic where we force every student to follow the same system. This obviously excludes medicine, law, and technology.

- Create an entrepreneurial experience where you find out early which kids gravitate toward entrepreneurship. I actually believe everyone is an entrepreneur from the natural artist to the kid who wants to be a real estate mogul. It's the mindset that needs to be taught early.

- Create low-cost online universities where anyone from around the world can get educated on any specific subject without the need to get a degree. Some of this exists today but mostly for STEM subjects and software coding.

Minimize:

- Minimize testing and increase hands-on activity. I've operated a sales organization for quite some time, and I can tell you that the best way to teach my leaders is by role playing. Nothing is more effective than that. Not a motivational speaker, or a manual. Whenever I take an audience of 100 and we role play for an hour straight, I not only have everyone's attention but at the same time, everyone is having fun while learning.

- Instead of making it a four-year bachelor's degree give the student the opportunity to obtain the degree in less time if four years is not needed. Frankly, I'd like to see a concentrated program that could be completed for some subjects in 18 months.

Increase:

- Increase education on life subjects that everyone will face such as marriage, parenting, seeking a job, how to do a job interview, people skills, leadership skills, taxes, politics, and others. Can you imagine how kids would respond if they were all required to go to the auditorium and watch three people from different political systems debate each other? Imagine a Republican, a Democrat and an independent debating the questions students and teachers ask that could lead the kids to make a decision for themselves.

Eliminate:

- Eliminate the mindset not to even try to change the system because it'll be too much work. Just like Apple constantly has their operating system update, it's time for us to question our educational system. We need to challenge our political leaders to listen to new innovative ways to enhance it before we become a laughing stock around the world for no longer having the best educational system.

Before you assume I am merely trying to offer a quick-fix that reduces the time and cost required to get a degree, I'd like to explore a related question: If we eliminate some of the current troves of general education courses, is there anything we should add to the curriculum? Are there topics that a well-informed citizenry should be taught? I'd like to offer my own list:

MARRIAGE

History proves that marriages that stay together, in terms of broad averages, produce children that do better in life than those from divorced homes. Divorce stats also show that divorce does not strengthen society. If that's the case, why not teach relationship skills as a general education course? Ask important questions such as "Why even get married?" to spur thought and discussion about this significant life decision.

Can anyone deny that people with better relational skills at home can take those skills to their job and community? No way. Thus, teaching marriage and relationship skills strengthens the person – and society.

PARENTING

Marriage typically, but not always, leads to children. There are many couples who choose not to have children or cannot have children. Some of these couples adopt or foster children, and some do not. When children do appear in a marriage or relationship, society benefits when they are raised properly and become good citizens. Any trip to an unsupervised daycare center will demonstrate that we run amok without guidance.

We all have sat in a restaurant or public place and observed children in need of guidance. On the one hand, we see parents who simply don't care. Those are a tragic lot because it's not the child's fault he or she does not receive good fundamental parenting. When he or she turns 18, however, the courts will not care that you received poor parenting. Drunk and disorderly conduct or soliciting an undercover cop will land you in the county jail. On the other hand, we see parents who are truly overwhelmed by the task at hand and would gladly accept help.

So, why not include parenting courses in the general education curriculum? You may say, "Don't be presumptive, not everyone wants children or will have children." You would be correct. BUT – can everyone be a good mentor or volunteer? YES! How many non-parents are actually an aunt or uncle? Parenting skills would help broader society, not just those who produce offspring of their own. It would also decrease the high school dropout rate, which would have a positive impact on society as well.

INDIVIDUAL INCOME TAXES & MONEY

If death and taxes are inevitable, why not teach about the principles of income tax and the implications of state and federal levies? I have had more than one CEO tell me that their HR department often counsels employees about income taxes. One such leader said to me, "There's generally a dearth of education out there, and the government isn't rushing to offer classes on how they take their share. At my company, we end up explaining tax code and implications to employees who approach HR and ask to adjust their withholdings to increase their take-home pay. We caution them and invariably ask tax experts to stand in front of our whiteboard explaining income taxes, FICA (Social Security), Medicare and state income tax. They appreciate the education and often comment, 'Where was the average person supposed to learn this stuff?'"

Students walk from college to their first full-time job where they will see more taxation than they saw at their part-time college job. It seems perfectly reasonable and appropriate that college should teach a general course about income taxes and taxation. This should be an unbiased explanation of "how" it works not an indoctrination into any particular political position.

THE IMPORTANCE OF VOTING

If you think the average person is uninformed about taxes, go visit your neighborhood Starbucks and have an impartial chat about voting. Few people understand how hard people worked to get women and minorities the right to vote. The history of voting and the importance of voting should be taught to all citizens. Just my opinion, of course.

POLITICS FROM BOTH SIDES

Let's face the truth – it's no small task to have an unbiased political dialogue. It's even tougher these days to have one with civility. Nonetheless, I believe we can and should teach our citizens about politics from both sides. For that matter, why not teach college students the SAME materials that immigrants are required to study to take the US citizenship test?

I once saw comedian Jay Leno interview people randomly on a city street and ask them the same questions that are on the citizenship test. The answers were humorous but also shocking. Why is it that the average person knows LESS about our government and political system than a newly minted citizen who immigrated legally from another country? It's because we don't teach it!

MORE PROOF

Would you like more evidence of the things that they should teach in college? A favorite management book of mine is *What They Don't Teach You at Harvard Business School* by Mark McCormack. The classic book covered many common-sense business topics and sat on the New York Times Best Seller List for many weeks. Why is that? I believe that the answer is simple: colleges teach topics as concepts and processes whereas common sense narrative from successful people is borne of their actual experience and such is not usually part of the typical curriculum.

LEADERSHIP

I'm not sure why we don't have an individual class titled leadership? This absolutely makes no sense to me. We're willing to teach kids how to dissect frogs which they'll probably never do in their lives, but we don't spend an entire semester teaching leadership, which they'll do the rest of their lives.

I can see this class teaching students different modes and styles of leadership that they can connect with and use in life. Leading at church, civic groups, charities and in their career!

There could be a diversity of styles versus rote traditional teachings. Sometimes, we feel we have to be like someone in order for us to be successful but this is a great opportunity for us to instill hope in our young adults to believe that even with their own quirky personality they can make a positive impact LEADING somewhere in their world.

TRADE SCHOOLS

Along the way, a case can and should be made for trade schools. The community college up the street from a friend in Denver has one of the best automotive programs in the nation. She indicated that nearly all the graduates already have a job waiting for them when they graduate and, of course, being a community college, it's inexpensive per course. Additionally, none of the courses in that type of program are fluff, they're all related to the degree, and they are generally two-year degrees since they're not packed with general education courses, such as astronomy.

Rather than adding automotive programs as a major to a larger university, trade schools sometimes thought of as a "last resort," are an alternative that is available today.

ONLINE EDUCATION

There is another emerging alternative that is already threatening computer science programs: online education. Startups including Cousera, Code Academy, and Udacity are helping those who dropped out of college or never attended in the first place, get jobs at Facebook, Google, and Twitter. Yep. Just code, baby!

In this emerging realm of online education, to date, the pure-play entrepreneur has not been well-served. I am about to change that with the launch of Entrepreneur University, "EU." EU will provide video courses for entrepreneurs taught by experts on key business topics including management, strategy, marketing, sales, fund-raising, finance, and accounting. We will also enable direct connections for video meetings between entrepreneurs and the experts who teach the classes.

I hope that this chapter has spurred thought. There are many things we can and should teach our citizens to help strengthen their skills and, in turn, our communities.

7

HOW TO PROCESS YOUR DECISION

Whatever you decide, know why you did it

"If you always make the right decision, the safe decision, the one most people make, you will be the same as everyone else."

— Paul Arden

As you consider your own situation, you may be someone who is looking for direction, or you may be someone reading this book to provide the best advice you possibly can.

Whoever you are, follow these steps to engage in a thoughtful debate that facilitates the process of helping someone make the important decision and OWN the outcome. The real debate is about not wasting your life. The purpose here is to ask the right questions, so you don't end up having a mid-life crisis at 44-years-old because you chose a route because that's what you thought you were supposed to do. At the same time, you also don't want to be 44 years old only making an average salary and struggling to keep things together with your family of four realizing how important of a role your income makes.

When we're younger, we feel more connected to social issues. We feel rich people are greedy. We want to see world peace take place. We want everyone to get along. We feel it's important to give everything away for free. We admire rock stars, athletes and anyone who at all comes across as a bit rebellious who wants to help make the weak stronger. Then as we age and any number of the following events take place, we tend to adjust our lens and even adjust our beliefs.

- Getting overlooked for a promotion or recognition by someone who doesn't work as hard as you but is great at the political game. If it hasn't happened yet, you are fortunate.

- When you decide to get your own place with a roommate and find out your roommate doesn't wash the dishes or do laundry. You do your part while your roommate makes the place smell.

- You have a boyfriend who makes you feel guilty if you don't pay for dinners because he's broke and can't find or keep a job.

- You try to bail out a friend by lending them money but realize they keep coming back for more money. Eventually, when you say no or ask them to pay you back, they get upset with you and call you names. In many cases that friendship ends up being ruined permanently.

- You get married and realize how expensive it is to raise a family. Nobody warned you about the normal life challenges of marriage and raising kids. You realize it's nothing like it's portrayed in movies.

- You start working late hours out of school for three years straight and miss many great moments with your family and friends and watch much of it go towards taxes. You start asking, Where do my taxes go? What do they do with it? How come the roads in my city haven't been updated for 20 years?

- You eventually realize that many of the political leaders on both sides of the aisle use the younger generation, and even the educational system itself, as a way to promote their agenda.

These are but a few of the events that change your lens and beliefs. The goal here is to challenge you to be aware and to question everything. Question the media on both sides. Question your parents' way of thinking. Question the next greatest social program. Not to be a sad cynic, but to be informed and know why you do what you do. To own and challenge your beliefs as a means of processing your positions, decisions, and beliefs. People who accept and never question the world around them are, in no small part, indoctrinated by the educational system which often teaches kids not to question "authority."

A productive way to process the college decision is to ask these questions:

1. What do I enjoy doing that I can see myself doing long term?

2. What can I do to maximize the amount of income I can make while doing this?

3. Do I need a college degree to do what I want to do?

4. Do I want to be an employee or an entrepreneur?

8

A SAMPLE CONVERSATION

It's not difficult to process your decision

*"The art of conversation is the art of hearing
as well as of being heard."*

— William Hazlitt,"

Where do you go from here? Clearly, if you are at the crossroads of life, it's time to process the decision about your own path; go to college, join the military, enroll in a trade school, start a business, join an early stage business or something else. Hopefully, you have a parent, trusted mentor or close friend, preferably with more life experience than you, to help you work through the alternatives as you come to your own decision.

At this juncture, I have asked Tom to offer a couple examples to help you envision your own "great debate" and subsequent decision. He has cleverly penned two conversations using his life as the canvas; one the NEVER happened and one that DID happen. I'll jump back in after you give these a read.

THE CONVERSATION THAT **DID** HAPPEN
In the Spring of 1980, I had not yet made up my mind about which college to attend. Nor had I truly processed the important decision about what subject I wanted to major in.

I enjoyed writing and story-telling and excelled in them to the point that keen-eyed teachers suggested to my parents that I consider applying those skills & competencies in a career in sales. I also maintained a large salt-water aquarium with many colorful fish in it and thanks, to the encouragement of my high school science teacher, I had volunteered to help rescue and protect sea turtles and their nests at the local beaches. Some of them were nurtured in my tank before returning to the wild. This led to love and appreciation for the ocean. These things combined to yield a rather impulsive and quite loosely considered decision to study Marine Biology or Creative Writing, but I was not fully resolved on either path. As you read in the Prologue, I was making reasonable money for a teenager in a local restaurant and had simultaneously opened a fledgling "business" repairing surfboards for a few surf shops.

Lurking in the background, some months earlier my dad had purchased "The Guide to US Colleges and Universities," to help spark discussions about my future. This book weighed several pounds and was the size of an old-school Yellow Pages phone book. Upon cursory review, I was somewhat intimidated by the scope and cost of the choices.

I didn't spend a lot of time on it, but I did look up schools that offered majors in Creative Writing and Marine Biology. I compared them to my SAT scores and high school GPA to see which ones would be likely to accept me. First, I looked up the top colleges offering creative writing degrees. These were mostly liberal arts colleges I had never heard of, such as Brandeis College in Massachusetts and Hamilton College in New York, and most of them seemed to be located in the Northeast. These schools were also fairly expensive which was going to be a problem. Neither my parents or I had significant resources.

I then looked up the top colleges that offered Marine Biology degrees. These included Woods Hole Institute in Massachusetts, Scripps Institute at UC San Diego and the University of Miami. Woods Hole sounded too cold, I had extended family in California, and I knew a little about the program at the University of Miami thanks to local environmental conservation efforts. As you can see, my decision process was not deep.

I found that it's one thing to look up a list of colleges, it's quite another to make a choice and pay for it. There was, however, a much bigger problem; I realized that not only was I not committed to Marine Biology or Creative Writing, but I also had no idea what I was actually committed to. I did know that it was gratifying and encouraging that surf shops lauded me for the repairs performed for their customers. I was self-conscious and insecure about my future and protected myself by not discussing these normal fears and apprehensions with anyone, even my close friends.

Not surprisingly, I had also avoided deeper conversations with my dad about my future because I found most of them frustrating. He would usually invoke his fatherly position, and I felt him guiding me through the lens of his own upbringing and situation (what other lens did he have?) rather than facilitating a conversation that ended with a decision that I owned. This experience has led me to be more self-aware and a much better career coach and mentor to people – but that's for another book.

Along the way, a friend of the family offered his advice – again from his personal lens. He was moving from IBM where Dad worked to a division of Schlumberger, a technology provider to the oil and gas exploration industry. He saw a bright future in petroleum engineering and enthusiastically encouraged me to apply to the University of Texas at Austin. While this made sense from a lot of angles, the guy in the middle was me, and I didn't fancy myself as an engineer.

On the other hand of the spectrum were older relatives, including a great aunt, who said: "many people wait a couple years to figure out life before they go to college." I noted that virtually nobody on her side of the family had attempted, let alone graduated from, college. As much as I loved her, the uninformed comments were summarily dispatched.

The point of those two examples is to show how many voices there are around us and rather than discount them, it's important to embrace them and process their perspectives as you make the choice that will be uniquely yours.

Back to my discussion about Marine Biology. Dad listened to me talk about my love for the sea and its creatures and my explanation that the University of Miami was top-rated and only an hour away from where we lived.

After my presentation, he casually asked me, "I know you *enjoy* fish and the ocean, but what exactly do you want to do with a degree in Marine Biology?"

I thought about it for a moment and admitted that I had not got that far. Dad then offered this key question, "Do any of the career options in Marine Biology interest you?" I sheepishly responded, "Actually, I don't know the full list of career options."

Unlike our discussions of the past, this one did not seem like I was being manipulated. Perhaps he was trying a different technique or perhaps I was a year older and beginning to listen or perhaps there was some combination of the two (Yep). Nevertheless, the question caused me, literally for the first time, to more completely process my decision about college through the lens of life beyond the last beer on graduation day.

At this point Dad offered a simple suggestion, "What do you think of this; contact the University of Miami placement office and ask them where most of the Marine Biology graduates go to work. I bet they'll have a list and be helpful." This seemed logical, and it didn't feel like he was hiding the answer, so I did.

Not only was the placement office helpful, but they were also extremely eager to passionately pitch the university's success helping marine biologist majors launch into fruitful careers. (Of course, the butcher said the meat was fresh!) I augmented the feedback from the university of Miami with what I could find out about marine biology careers in general.

The results of this research, however, were not something that excited me. A large percentage of bachelor degree graduates continued in school and earned a Master's degree. In turn, a very large percentage of Master's graduates went on to earn a Ph.D. If you didn't embark on this seemingly eternal educational path, the number of jobs was limited and, frankly, not very exciting. In writing this book, I also took the time to research the same question again and, not at all surprisingly, the answer has NOT changed in 20 years! The following is provided this year (2016) by NOAA (National Oceanic Atmospheric Administration) regarding the future for Marine Scientists – the title afforded individuals earning a degree in Marine Biology:

"The employment outlook in this field is highly competitive. The supply of marine scientists far exceeds the demand, and the number of government jobs is limited. Other employers are aquaria/museums, colleges and universities, and private research laboratories or consulting firms."

Before sharing the results with my dad, I did a little additional research and decoded the list of jobs:

Government Jobs: Public Policy Officials making laws and regulations about the rivers, coasts, and oceans.

Colleges / Universities: Professors who are teaching the next generation of marine biologists.

Aquaria / Museums: Staff tasked with taking care of the fish and animals on display for the public.

Private Research / Consulting Firms: Lobbyists for Oil Companies drilling off-shore who often appear in court as expert witnesses and argue with Public Policy Officials.

I carefully considered the above list and in a bit of rather shallow thinking surmised; "Wait for a second, where's the job where you get to date cute women because you love dolphins?" I concluded that clearly, those women are probably not attracted to a policy wonk working in Washington DC and even less interested in an expert witness lobbying for an oil company. The answer to a "fun" career seemed to be a gig at Seaworld. But, I had already read articles about their questionable environments and treatment of sea animals along with the occasional Orca / Killer Whale that would injure a trainer. Keep in mind this was only 1980, and things have become even worse as several trainers have been killed by captive Orcas, exposing even more serious issues at SeaWorld.

OK, so beyond my shallow thinking (remember, I was 18), I already knew I didn't click with environmentalist types who were out to save some rare snail. And beyond that, NONE of those "real jobs" interested me in the least.

When Dad and I restarted the conversation, he listened to my findings and asked another very simple question, "I think I sense the answer but do you find any of those career options exciting?"

My answer was a quick and emphatic, "No way."

He replied, "Then continue the journey to figure out what you want to do." He paused for effect and continued, "You can always go diving on vacations to interesting places and visit aquariums that do good work."

I felt a sense of relief and said, "You're right."

"Tom, there's one more thing."

"What's that, Dad?"

He smiled and said, "Take that huge aquarium when you move out. It's nice, but please take the smell with you."

I was somewhat shocked. "Wait, I thought you liked fish?"

"I do. They taste good with lemon and butter."

I still had no idea what I wanted to do but definitely knew that a career in marine biology was NOT what I wanted. Further, this simple exercise taught me how to process my decision. In case you are wondering, Creative Writing would be quickly ruled out because the thought of being a starving author or newspaper reporter was unappealing. The world needs authors and reporters, but I was not going to be one of them.

Over the course of the next several months, I would reach the conclusion that there was not a scientific avenue that interested me, such as medicine. I expanded my surfboard repair business – and then closed it when Dad kicked me out of the garage. Along the way, I used the skills learned to repair surfboards to refinish a bar at a restaurant and repair a ski boat. I enjoyed word of mouth and was opportunistic about my little business.

It is from this perspective that I concluded that a degree in business would provide me a broad set of skills that I could apply in a range of industries. I'll skip the details, but this led to receiving a Bachelor's of Science in Business with an emphasis in Marketing followed by an MBA. In an ironic twist, the MBA was earned at Pepperdine University, in Malibu California on the coast of the Pacific Ocean.

– TNE

THE CONVERSATION THAT **NEVER** HAPPENED

In the fall of 1979, my dad approached me and asked if we might sit down and have a chat.

He began, "Tom, it's time to start a dialogue that will not end today. In fact, it will very likely be months before we even reach the first milestone. Still, it's time to talk about life and decisions after high school."

"Dad, I have ideas, but I don't have a firm view."

He smiled, "That's not a problem – in fact, it's pretty normal. If you had a strong opinion, we'd test it, and you'd probably find that it wasn't as strong as you thought."

"OK, I get it."

"Let me start with what I see, not what I want for you, just what I objectively see."

I was suspicious but allowed him to continue.

"Obviously, you have a unique set of skills. First, you are quantitative and logical in your approach to things. Second, you are very resourceful and fearlessly creative in developing solutions to problems, but not creative like an artist. Third, you process numbers and issues very quickly, which amplifies the effectiveness of your logic skills. Fourth, you enjoy working with your hands which is evident in the surfboard repair business you built out of nothing and working on your car, although the latter may be because it's cheaper to change your oil and brakes yourself. Fifth, you truly enjoy English and some science classes but mostly tolerate math."

As I listened it was clear he was paying attention, and this led to me trusting what he was saying.

"So, that said, there are a number of ways to get an education. You can go straight to college or join the military and use the GI Bill to go to college when your enlistment is over. You can also go to trade school and become an electrician or something similar, but I don't get the impression that's an angle you find interesting."

I said, "No it's not" and began to process what he was saying regarding education. Dad wasn't assuming that an immediate enrollment in college was automatic. I also knew he wasn't an entrepreneur and, thus, didn't have that experience and coming from a divorced home of meager means he prioritized security over risk. On the other hand, I read about "self-made men" and thought it was both exciting and meaningful.

Dad continued, "I'd like to point out that I'm not sure the surfboard business you are operating out of my garage is something to make a career out of, given that you are not making enough to pay employees, rent or other normal expenses. You have done a nice job hustling, and I think it's been a nice experience for you and it has shown me you have a nose for your own business."

I appreciated the perspective and knew that he was correct. "Yeah, but Dad, I have made some good money."

He nodded in agreement. "Sure you have, but that is a bit of an illusion in the face of what it would really take to run an end-to-end business."

"So, how should I approach the bigger question? I honestly don't have a firm idea about a college major but have thought about Creative Writing and Marine Biology."

At that point he shifted gears, "I'd like to see you process those thoughts through a longer-term view of what you would do, how applicable are the skills we both know you have and other majors you may not be thinking of, including general business."

"Where do I start?" I was now interested and felt like I was in charge of the decision versus being lectured.

"Maybe go take a look at the passion you have for creative writing and marine biology. Do you *enjoy* those things or do you have a *passion for working* in those areas – there's a huge difference. For example, everyone loves puppies, but very few people have a passion for running a kennel or breeder as a business. Such a business requires that you care for puppies 24 X 7, train them, endlessly clean up after them and sometimes watch helplessly as sick ones die despite the best medication and care."

That example struck me, and I instantly began questioning whether I enjoyed marine biology or had a passion for it as a profession. In other words, I had the first item on my to-do list.

"That makes so much sense and seems so obvious. I wish I had thought of that."

He smiled and said, "That's what mentors are for, and while I am your dad, I am also called to be your mentor. But if I weren't here, hopefully, some other voice or mentor would be sharing this with you."

"Is there anything else I should do?"

"Yes, take some notes and tell me what you enjoy about the surfboard repair business. Do you like the outcome, the work, the look on the faces of your customers or just the money? Be specific and let's go over those notes next weekend. Hopefully, you'll have some answers or more questions about the other things we discussed."

This began a journey which encompassed two months of conversations, research, and opinions from a couple of trusted friends. At the conclusion, I made what was, up to that point, the most important decision of my life; I chose to attend college and get a business degree while interning for free each summer with a prominent entrepreneur.

— TNE

What did you think of that? Was that thoughtful? Did you feel the emotion and the weight of the decision? Can you see yourself being a parent or a mentor like Tom's dad? Can you see yourself being honest with yourself like Tom?

Your answer may not be college – it may be the military, trade school, a certification program or community college. The point here is to be diligent, objective and find *your answer*. As long as you are doing your best with the situation you are in and the resources available to you, you can and should be proud of your answer. Your answer is uniquely yours, applies best to you and should never be compared to others or denigrated in any way.

Use Chapter 8 as your guide and start processing your decision. Enjoy the journey and look to the exciting future that is uniquely yours.

9

WHAT NOW?
JOIN THE DROP OUT REVOLUTION!

Whether you agree or disagree with this book, the purpose is to start the conversation. Change starts with an open dialogue and I WANT to hear from you.

If you are wondering what to do next, here are a few suggestions:

1. **Make a YouTube video** sharing your thoughts. Please name the video this way, and we'll add it to our playlist:

   "Drop Out and Get Schooled - YOUR NAME, YOUR CITY"

2. **Gift this book** or tell 5 people about it. Such as:

   a. Friend

   b. Parent

   c. Teacher

   d. Influencer

   e. Government official (Parole Officer doesn't count)

3. **Take a picture of this book**, or a selfie with it, and share it on social media with the hashtag **#dropoutbook**

Join the dialogue! Please visit www.dropoutbook.com and post your ideas about how you would change the educational system.

ADDENDUM

DROPOUT HALL OF FAME
(They Didn't Merely Get Lucky)

*"Your time is limited,
so don't waste it living someone else's life.*

Don't be trapped by dogma - which is living with the results of other people's thinking.

Don't let the noise of other's opinions drown out your own inner voice.

And most important, have the courage to follow your heart and intuition. They somehow already know what you truly want to become.

Everything else is secondary."

– Steve Jobs

We all know that Steve Jobs and Bill Gates dropped out of college. There are many notable individuals that dropped out of college. When we peel back the onion and take a look at many of them, it's clear they had a few things in common.

First, they knew exactly why they were dropping out or were

not going to college in the first place. They all had a vision and passion for doing something amazing. Their vision came with a plan, and that plan was to get going NOW instead of staying in school.

In 2009, John Carney of Business Insider made such a list of famous college dropouts and summarized their accomplishments. It was a quite impressive article. Let's take a look at his list: I

Paul Allen

Paul Allen attended Washington State University for just two years before dropping out.

Accomplishments: Allen co-founded Microsoft in 1975 with Bill Gates, whom he convinced to drop out of Harvard. In addition to his stake in Microsoft, Allen owns a dozen professional sports teams and has stakes in technology and media companies such as DreamWorks Studios.

Richard Branson

Richard Branson left school when he was only 16 and never returned.

Accomplishments: Branson has built his brand Virgin—which includes Virgin Records, Virgin Atlantic Airways, and many other companies, into an international powerhouse that has driven his personal wealth into the billions.

Michael Dell

Michael Dell started a computer company called "PCs Limited" while attending the University of Texas at Austin. He dropped out of school to operate it.

Accomplishments: Dell's company was later renamed Dell, Inc., with revenues and enterprise valuation deep into the tens of billions.

Larry Ellison

Larry Ellison is actually a two-time dropout. He went to both the University of Illinois and the University of Chicago. But he never got a degree.

Accomplishments: Ellison put up $2,000 in 1977 to start what would become Oracle Corporation, the world's second-largest software company. It became THE standard for enterprise-grade databases. He also used his wealth to parlay his passion for yacht racing into an entry into the America's Cup, which his boat won.

David Geffen

David Geffen never attended college.

Accomplishments: Geffen is widely known as one of Hollywood's richest men. He founded Asylum Records and Geffen Records and later built DreamWorks with Steven Spielberg.

Mike Hudack

Mike Hudack left high school and never attended college

Accomplishments: Hudack is the founder and CEO of blip.tv, a hosting platform for creators of digital video content. Blip is now backed by venture capital, including Bain Capital Ventures.

Dean Kamen

After attending Worcester Polytechnic Institute for a couple of years, Dean Kamen dropped out before graduating.

Accomplishments: Kamen holds more than 80 US patents, and is the inventor of the Segway. He also is a pioneer in prosthetics that are enabling US military veterans to recover from wartime injuries.

David Karp

David Karp dropped out of the elite Bronx High School of Science when he was 15. After two more years of homeschooling, he moved to Tokyo.

Accomplishments: Karp went on to found Tumblr, the blog hosting, and social network company.

Ralph Lauren

Ralph Lauren studied business for two years at Baruch College before dropping out.

Accomplishments: He founded Polo Ralph Lauren a fashion empire. He's why you have the pony on some of your shirts.

Kirk Kerkorian

Kirk Kerkorian dropped out of school in the 8th grade.

Accomplishments: Kerkorian has been one of the most important shapers of Las Vegas, and currently has a large stake in some of the most prestigious hotels in Vegas: Bellagio, Excaliber, Luxor, Mandalay Bay, MGM Grand, New York-New York, Circus Circus, and The Mirage.

Kevin Rose

Kevin Rose dropped out of the University of Nevada, Las Vegas in 1998.

Accomplishments: Rose used money planned for a down payment on a house with his (now ex) girlfriend to start the website Digg.

Jack Taylor

When World War II broke out, Jack Taylor dropped out of college and joined the Navy to be a fighter pilot.

Accomplishment: He founded Enterprise Rent-A-Car and is still running the business.

YC Wang

YC Wang never got further than elementary school education.

Accomplishments: Despite humble beginnings as the son of a tea farmer in Taiwan, Wang went on to make Formosa Plastics into one of Asia's largest Petrochemical producers.

Mark Zuckerberg

Mark Zuckerberg dropped out of Harvard after starting a social networking site in his dorm room in 2004.

Accomplishments: The social networking site he founded is Facebook. Hmmm. Not bad.

Travis Kalanick

Travis Kalanick dropped out of UCLA while studying computer engineering and joined a peer-to-peer technology company. It allowed people to share music and videos and went bankrupt after being sued by almost every company in the movie and music industry. He started a new company, and after five years of trying to go big, it was sold to Akamai for "only" $20 Million dollars.

Accomplishments: A decade after dropping out of UCLA and "getting educated" by failure and real-world experience, he became CEO of Uber. Five years later it was worth over $30 Billion and is revolutionizing instant transportation and delivery of people, things, and food while helping to fuel the "gig economy."

ABOUT THE AUTHORS

Patrick Bet-David

Patrick's amazing story starts with his family immigrating to America when he was 10-years old. His parents fled Iran as refugees during the Iranian revolution and were eventually granted U.S. citizenship.

After high school, Patrick joined the U.S. military and served in the 101st Airborne before starting a business career in the financial services industry. After a tenure with a couple of traditional companies, he was inspired to launch PHP Agency Inc., an insurance sales, marketing, and distribution company – and did so before he turned 30. PHP is now one of the fastest growing companies in the financial marketplace.

Patrick is passionate about shaping the next generation of leaders by teaching thought-provoking perspectives on entrepreneurship and disrupting the traditional approach to a career. Patrick's popularity surged and created a buzz in the hearts of entrepreneurs all over the world when The Life of an Entrepreneur in 90 Seconds, a video he created, accumulated over 28+ million views online (It became a book in June 2016: *The Life of an Entrepreneur in 90 Pages*). That video and scores of other videos comprise his library of edifying, educational and inspirational content about entrepreneurship – all available at Valuetainment, a media brand he conceived and founded.

Valuetainment exists to teach the fundamentals of entrepreneurship and personal development while inspiring people to break free from limiting beliefs or other constraints and achieve their dreams. It has been referred to as "the voice for entrepreneurs."

Patrick speaks on a range of business, leadership and entrepreneurial topics including how and why to become an entrepreneur and the importance of learning how to process issues fully. He is particularly passionate about the need for every individual to pursue their desires, once stating, "Most of the greatest world changers and heroes of all time are at the graveyard undiscovered because they never sold out to their dreams and desires."

Patrick has also hosted a series of one-on-one interviews with some of the world's most interesting people, including NBA Hall of Famer James Worthy, author Robert Greene, billionaire and entrepreneur Mark Cuban, Indy-500 winner Al Unser Jr., Apple co-founder, Steve Wozniak, author and entrepreneur Robert Kiyosaki, and many others.

From a humble beginning as a young immigrant escaping war-torn Iran with his parents to founding his own company, Patrick has gained a first-hand understanding of what rags-to-riches means and how it is fueled by freedom and opportunity – the core tenants of the American Dream.

Patrick resides in Dallas, TX with his wife and three children. You can learn more about Patrick, his books, and the library of Valuetainment content at:

www.patrickbetdavid.com

Thomas N. Ellsworth

Tom is an experienced CEO, C-Level mentor & author with a passion for teaching, mentorship and professional development that drives his credo; "Leave People Better Than You Found Them."

A veteran entrepreneur, Ellsworth's first start-up was a surfboard repair business that took over the garage at his parents' house. The thriving business closed when his parents essentially evicted him and sent him to college.

Following college, he began a career that has enabled him to be part of Venture-backed and mid-stage companies that have generated transactions/exits totaling over $1B.

Currently, Ellsworth is President and COO of PHP Agency Inc. where he works with Patrick Bet-David on a crusade to change the life insurance industry, mentor entrepreneurs and change the face of education.

Previously Ellsworth was CEO and Chairman of Premier Digital Publishing, "PDP," an eBook publisher and technology developer that put seven titles on the New York Times bestseller list in under two years and was acquired by a large New York publisher in 2014.

Before PDP, Ellsworth was CEO of GoTV Networks, a provider of rich media applications. GoTV was the go-to partner for brands and media owners including the NFL, Verizon, Sprint, Oprah and NASCAR. Ellsworth led the company through a complete financial and strategic turnaround followed by a successful acquisition in 2011.

Prior to GoTV, Ellsworth served as Executive Vice President, Marketing, and Corporate Development at JAMDAT Mobile. Inc. (NASDAQ: JMDT), the largest wireless games publisher in the world. He was a core member of the senior management team that drove the company from start-up to its highly successful IPO (later acquired by Electronic Arts).

In advance of JAMDAT, he was Vice President of the eCompanies Wireless Startup Incubator, a Corporate Venture Capital project for Sprint. He managed the fund that identified and invested in start-up companies including JAMDAT, Boingo, and Helio.

He received his Bachelor of Science degree in Business Administration; Marketing from California State University, Northridge and an MBA from Pepperdine University.

Today, Tom calls Dallas, Texas home along with his wife – a teacher, and their two children. You can visit Tom and see his library of business books and visit his blog at:

www.tomellsworth.com

SPEAKING REQUESTS

To inquire about speaking requests, please send an email with information about the engagement including date, location, size of audience and any other details to marketing@patrickbetdavid.com

PATRICK BET-DAVID with THOMAS N. ELLSWORTH

END NOTES

[i] The National Center for Education Statistics: Digest of Education statistics.
https://nces.ed.gov/programs/digest/d15/tables/dt15_326.10.asp

[ii] http://www.skilledup.com/articles/college-graduate-sales-job

[iii] http://www.huffingtonpost.com/amy-rosen/colleges-face-challenges-_b_9131860.html

[iv] http://www.cheatsheet.com/personal-finance/5-reasons-why-you-shouldnt-go-to-college.html

[v] http://ryanholiday.net/how-dropping-out-of-college-can-save-your-life-2/

[vi] http://fortune.com/2016/03/08/mount-st-marys-firing-simon-newman/

[vii] http://www.nbcnews.com/business/business-news/students-are-still-saddled-soaring-textbook-costs-report-says-n516011

[viii] http://time.com/money/4508221/iphone-7-mark-up-profit-margins/

[ix] http://www.huffingtonpost.com/sean-kim/how-i-went-from-dropping-out-of-college-to-freedom-in-two-years_b_6264140.html

Printed in Great Britain
by Amazon

46756272R00078